Hervey's Boys: New Jersey's First Chinese Community 1870-1886

(And What Happened After That)

Additional books by author:

Firehouse Fraternity Oral History Series:
Volume I: Becoming a Firefighter
Volume II: Life Between Alarms
Volume III: Equipment
Volume IV: Responding
Volume V: Riots to Renaissance
Volume VI: Changing the NFD

The Newark Riots: A View from the Firehouse

An Eerie Silence: An Oral History of Newark Firefighters at the WTC

Fiction:
The Firebox Stalker
The Hand Life Dealt you
A-zoe: A Woman Living in Interesting Times

Children's Fiction:
A Hundred Battles (YA)
A Broken Glass (YA)
Balancing Act (Middle Grade)

Hervey's Boys: New Jersey's First Chinese Community 1870-1886

(And What Happened After That)

Neal Stoffers

Springfield and Hunterdon Publishing
Copyright 2019
www.newarkfireoralhistory.com

Copyright © 2019 by Neal Stoffers

All rights reserved. This book or any portion thereof may not be reproduced or used in any manner whatsoever without the express written permission of the publisher except for the use of brief quotations in a book review or scholarly journal.

First Printing: 2019

ISBN 978-1-970034-26-4

Springfield and Hunterdon Publishing
East Brunswick, NJ 08816

To Miaoli, Will, and Joy

Contents

FOREWORD i
PREFACE 1
ARRIVAL 4
REACTION TO THE CHINESE 10
THE CHINESE AND POLITICS 16
LIFE IN THE CHINESE COLONY 23
NEWSPAPER COVERAGE 354
INTERACTING WITH THE OUTSIDE WORLD 387
AMERICAN IGNORANCE AND OPPOSITION 421
THE LUNAR NEW YEAR 465
CHINESE EXCLUSION 565
CONTINUING AMERICANIZATION 587
THE END OF THE FIRST CHINESE COMMUNITY ... 632
BECOMING PART OF AMERICA 665
Appendixes 80
Bibliography 83

FOREWORD

My interest in New Jersey's first Chinese community began with a short research paper. I decided on this topic after reading a few books on the Chinese experience in California. One of these books mentioned something about Chinese laborers being sent to Belleville, New Jersey. There was, however, very little information about these Chinese workers included in this book. I had been born and raised in New Jersey, but was unaware of this early Chinese colony that was located a few miles from my home. The topic was both fascinating and challenging, although I doubted I could find enough material to complete a twenty page paper. In the end I submitted a twenty-five page paper which only sparingly covered the first ten years the Chinese were in the state. I also discovered a need.

This need became evident very early in my research. I found that there were almost no secondary sources on this subject, only a few inaccurate articles on the early years of the Chinese in New Jersey. When I inquired at libraries in the area I received encouragement, but little information.

I started my research with some very basic questions. When and where did the Chinese first arrive in New Jersey? How many Chinese arrived in that first group? How were they treated? How long did this first colony exist?

Even the simplest of these questions, "When did the Chinese first arrive in New Jersey?" was unclear. Dates for the arrival of the Chinese varied. One source claimed they arrived in 1870. Another source claimed the Chinese arrived in 1872. Still another was sure they did not come to the Garden State until 1874. The number of Chinese men who made up that first group ranged from 50 to 300, depending on which of these sources one used. Even the location of the steam laundry where they first worked was confused. *

It is appropriate that someone with my background should try to answer these questions. Since I was a native of northern New Jersey, I am familiar with the localities I would have to write about. A second advantage I had was my academic background. My concentration has been China. This gave me an understanding of the cultural environment the subjects of my research came from.

Even with this academic background, researching this topic has been a learning experience. The language, history, and culture I have spent years studying are from northern China. The Chinese who formed this earliest of Chinese communities in New Jersey were predominantly from Canton Province in the southeast. They were not from the "great tradition" taught in American universities, but from the "small tradition" which existed thousands of miles south of the Chinese capital. Theirs was not the world of dynasties rising and falling, but of the farm in Toisan or Canton County. The language they spoke was unintelligible in the north. They were, for the most

---

* These secondary sources included a paper written for a Federal Writers Project in 1932 as a history of Belleville. An article using this source was written for the North Jersey Highlander Historical Society magazine *The North Jersey Highlander* in September, 1973. Another source was an article printed in the magazine supplement to the *Belleville Times* of April 17, 1969. The North Arlington City Clerk (Connie Meehan) provided me with a history of the town and a short article concerning the history of the buildings of the Passaic Laundry.

part, Cantonese peasants who came to the Golden Mountain to earn and save as much money as possible, so they might support their families in China. I tried to write their story as they might have experienced it day to day. That is how they lived. While China was in the turmoil of dynastic change, these men simply worked, saved, and dreamed of their home villages.

From the beginning of my research it was obvious I would have to ignore secondary sources and build my own "data base". The information I needed on the early history of the Chinese in New Jersey would have to come from news accounts of the 19th century.

As with any historical study, this subject cannot be divorced from events outside the area of the study's concentration. Attitudes in Congress affected legislation that ultimately led to passage of the Chinese Exclusion Act of 1882. Opportunities or the lack of opportunities throughout the country affected the number of Chinese in New Jersey. The opinions of people outside the Garden State could affect the opinions of many of its citizens. In order to get an accurate picture of events in New Jersey and how the Chinese might have viewed them, national events needed to be considered.

I set out to write as detailed an account as possible. I wanted to record what it was like to live in this early community. What were the hopes, fears, frustrations, and triumphs of New Jersey's first Chinese residents? How were those who emigrated from the world's oldest continuous civilization treated in the Garden State?

I do not want to make the impression that this study concerns a large segment of the population of New Jersey. It does not. Because of the Chinese Exclusion Acts in effect between 1882 and 1943, the number of Chinese in New Jersey was never great. It must be kept in mind, however, that since the passage of immigration reform in 1965 the Chinese population in New Jersey has been expanding rapidly. I hope this study will tell these new immigrants something of what it was like for the first Chinese who lived in New Jersey.

PREFACE

China in 1870 was in the throes of dynastic change. The alien Qing Dynasty (1644-1911) had reached its zenith in 1795 when the Qian Long Emperor abdicated the dragon throne. The following year the country was struck by the first of a series of ever worsening peasant rebellions. Between 1762 and 1846 the population had doubled, but the amount of arable land could not keep pace. This disparity caused the cost of rented land to skyrocket. These increases squeezed the already stressed peasant population. Contact with European nations only made matters worse.

Distance had always insulated China from the cultures on the western extreme of the Eurasian land mass. Contacts between East and West were relatively limited. All of this changed when trade began between Great Britain and China. The English love of Chinese teas caused a serious trade imbalance to develop. The Chinese insisted on payments in silver from the UK which had nothing the Chinese wished to purchase. This caused an outflow of silver bullion from Great Britain to China. Finding the situation intolerable, the English shipped opium to China from their newly acquired colony, India.

In 1839 China confiscated barrels of opium and triggered a war. The First Opium war went badly for China. When it ended in 1842, she had lost Hong Kong Island and was forced to open ports for trade with the West. The Tai-ping Rebellion (1850-1868) came close to toppling the dynasty. But it was not the only unrest the Qing had to face in this period. The Manchu dynasty also had to deal with the Nien Rebellion (1851-1868), the Moslem Rebellion (1855-1873) and a second war with Great Britain (Arrow affair) in 1856. The peasant farmers of Guangdong province were hard pressed. When word of the discovery of gold in California reach them, dreams of striking it rich in the "Golden Mountain" and returning to China with enough cash to purchase a farm pulled many young men away from their home.

The country they were going to was young and brash, filled with immigrants from the old world and changing rapidly. The Civil War (1861-1865) had only ended five years before. German and Irish immigrants were pouring into the country. News of gold in California in 1849 had only heightened the push to America. Along with the challenge of absorbing so many people from different cultures, came the task of Reconstruction (1865-1877). Technology was increasing the pace change. Steam ships cut travel time from the old world to the new substantially. The completion of the transcontinental railroad in 1869 pulled the nation closer together. Chinese labor had built the westernmost portion of the railroad over the Sierra Nevada Mountains. Yet the Naturalization Law of 1870 targeted these same workers, excluding all Asians from the naturalization process.

The New Jersey of 1870 had a population of 906,096 with 188,943 being foreign born. The Irish and Germans made up the largest proportion of these, but the state remained predominantly Anglo-Saxon and Protestant. Newark, the state's largest city, was developing into an industrial powerhouse. A few miles to the north, the village of Belleville had a mixed economy including farms and a steam laundry, Major Blewett's Belleville Laundry. The economy of the state was moving away from a predominantly agrarian one dominated by small farms (The Garden State). Colgate was founded in Jersey City in 1847, Campbell's in Camden in 1869, Singer in Elizabeth in 1873, Prudential in Newark in 1873, Johnson and Johnson in New Brunswick in 1873, Mennen in Newark in 1879, and Thomas Edison was in Menlo Park (1876-1886) and West Orange (1886-1931). New Jersey's first Chinese stepped into this boiling caldron of change.

ARRIVAL

On the morning of September 20, 1870 the southbound Number 6 train on the Erie Railroad pulled into the Port Jervis New York station. When the train continued its southward journey later that morning, it was two cars shorter. Aboard the two cars left behind in Port Jervis were sixty-eight Chinese men. They had begun their journey from San Francisco, California two weeks earlier.[1]

It was not until after nightfall that these cars began the last leg of their journey, crossing the New Jersey state-line. The ultimate destination of the Chinese laborers was the Passaic Steam Laundry. Described as the "most extensive of its kind in the country", the laundry was located on a little over four acres of land in a "quite rural district . . . just opposite Belleville."[2]

---

[1] *Newark Evening Courier*, September 21, 1870; *Newark Daily Advertiser*, September 22, 1870; *New York Herald*, September 23, 1870; *Newark Daily Journal*, September 22, 1870. As for the discrepancy in numbers of the Chinese actually arriving or employed at the Passaic Steam Laundry, it was not until after George Casebolt took over the laundry in 1875 that the inflated number of 300 began to appear.

[2] *Newark Daily Advertiser*, September 22, 1870; *New York Herald*, September 22, 1870; *New Daily Journal*, September 22, 1870. This last article put the laundry in Hudson County; it is actually in Bergen County. The Passaic Steam Laundry was never located in Belleville, but in present day North Arlington. It appears that some have confused the North Arlington laundry with the Belleville Steam Laundry. The newspapers of the time always referred to the Passaic Steam Laundry as being in Belleville. The Belleville Steam Laundry was located along the Passaic River in Belleville and was owned by William Blewett. I will continue to use Belleville as the location of the Passaic Steam Laundry because newspaper accounts of the times place it there. This will avoid confusion. The size of the

The owner of this laundry, Captain James B. Hervey, had gone to San Francisco two months earlier looking for a solution to the labor problems that had plagued his business. Hervey, a former sea captain, had been in the laundry business for twenty-five years, seventeen of these in Belleville. Prior to his trip to California, he had obtained most of the workers for his laundry from among newly arrived Irish immigrant women at the Castle Garden landing depot in New York City. This workforce had proved to be both temperamental and transient.[3]

Although frustrating for the Captain, it should not have surprised him. The average girl working at Hervey's was in her twenties and single. She would probably be more interested in marriage than in a career as a laundrywoman. Captain Hervey complained that he had "found it impossible to depend on female labor - the girls were always off at picnics or parties of some kind." Many of the girls Hervey recruited would leave his establishment shortly after being trained. Those who remained would go on strike for higher wages as soon as they learned their employer had signed a large contract. Hervey claimed he had "often been compelled to refuse a great deal of work from New York" because of the nature of his workers. He estimated

---

property was obtained at the Bergen County Clerk, Registry Office, Book O-9 page 39. The deed recorded on this page is dated August 4, 1875. Since there were no other purchases or sales of property by James Hervey between 1870 and 1875, I am assuming the size of this property remained constant throughout the period.

[3]*Newark Daily Journal*, September 19, 1870, September 21, 1870, September 22, 1870; *New York Herald*, September 23, 1870.

that he had lost $10,000 the previous year because of this. To add to his frustrations, Captain Hervey found it increasingly difficult to find women willing to work for him. It was his hope that adding Chinese laborers to his workforce would bring some stability to it.[4]

When Hervey arrived in San Francisco, he sought out the Chinese labor broker Cornelius Koopmanschap. Unfortunately for the Captain, Koopmanschap had gone East to see how an experiment with Chinese labor begun earlier that year in North Adams, Massachusetts was progressing. Undaunted by his bad luck, Hervey next went to see George Sanford. Sanford had managed a workforce of 10,000 Chinese laborers who had helped build the Central Pacific Railroad. Sanford sent the Captain to 733 Commercial Street between Dupont and Kearny Streets. Here Hervey spoke with a labor broker named Ah Young. From him he received the promise of seventy-five Chinese men who would be willing to sign a contract to work in the New Jersey steam laundry for three years. Ah Young received $1 per man for his efforts. In addition to this money, Hervey provided $120.00 per man to defray the cost of travel. He then boarded a fast

---

[4]*New York Herald*, September 23, 1870; *Newark Daily Journal*, September 21, 1870, September 22, 1870; *U.S. Census 1870*, Union Township, N.J., of the 50 girls listed 5 are teenagers and 36 are in their twenties; *N.J. State Census 1855*, Union Township. There seems to be some confusion as to whether Captain Hervey was a retired sea Captain or a veteran of the Civil War. He appears in the *N. J. State Census* as Captain Hervey in 1855. I would be hesitant to use the word retired in describing Hervey, he was only 37 years of age in 1855. He apparently began the laundry business in New York, or at least that is where his wife and first two children were born. His third child was born in New Jersey and was four years old when the census was taken in June of 1860.

train to New Jersey. The Captain spoke with railroad officials along the way to ensure a smooth trip for his new employees. Seven of the men Ah Young had hired were frightened off by a $3 exit tax imposed on the Chinese as they were leaving California. The other sixty-eight men left San Francisco during the first week of September.[5]

From his actions after he returned to New Jersey, it is apparent Captain Hervey was aware of what happened in North Adams when the Chinese laborers had arrived there. The people of that New England village had known the arrival time of the train carrying the Chinese men. When "the train arrived . . . the depot square was thronged with an excited crowd of citizens." Hervey feared a repetition of this scene because of threats he had received. He did all he could to prevent it. When Hervey was asked on September 17 about a rumor that he was importing fifty Chinese laborers to replace the workers at his laundry he denied it. He also arranged to have the cars carrying the Chinese men delayed in Port Jervis. This ensured they would arrive in Belleville after dark. A fence was then erected around the laundry grounds to prevent any interaction between the Chinese laborers and "too curious visitors."[6]

The Cantonese men disembarked from the train "at Santiago Park . . . about a quarter mile from Passaic Bridge." Because of a

---

[5]*Newark Daily Journal*, September 22, 1870; *New York Herald*, September 23, 1870; *Newark Evening Courier*, September 28, 1870.

[6]*Newark Evening Courier*, September 17, 1870; *Newark Daily Journal*, September 22, 1870; *Newark Daily Advertiser*, September 22, 1870; *New York Times*, August 8, 1880.

mix-up in telegraph messages, the Captain was unsure of the arrival time of the train. Thus, the wagons he had intended for use in transporting his new laborers and their luggage to the laundry were not at the station. The luggage of the Chinese had to be left at the depot until the following morning. The new arrivals walked to the laundry. It was "just midnight when the Chinese walked down the empty streets of Belleville to quarters prepared for them." They arrived at the laundry about one o'clock.[7]

When the Chinese awoke the following day they found themselves the center of attention. A Newark newspaper announced that the "heathen Chinese . . . had invaded the sacred soil of New Jersey" in its evening issue of September 22. Rumors and speculation about the newly arrived laborers were published daily for the next few days. There were reports of an imminent riot between the Chinese and Irish workers, of 150 Chinese men arriving to work on the Midland Railroad, and of the Chinese replacing all the Irish women employed at the laundry. One paper stated the report of the Chinese taking the place of the women at the laundry is likely to be correct, for the Chinese are especially fond of washing clothes . . .." Captain Hervey found it necessary to tell the press he did not "intend to discharge any of his present employees . . .." He explained that the

---

[7]*Newark Evening Courier*, September 21, 1870; *Newark Daily Journal*, September 22, 1870; *Jersey City Evening Courier*, September 22, 1870; *Newark Daily Advertiser*, September 22, 1870.

Chinese were brought in "only as auxiliaries."[8]

Reporters swarmed the laundry "to view and interview the Celestial strangers." The tone of the reports printed in the Newark press varied. One paper described the members of the newly formed colony as "young and intelligent." Another stated the recent arrivals were better looking than the Chinese in New York City, but some "preserve a stupid expression of countenance."[9]

A reporter who walked through the living quarters of the Chinese saw the Cantonese men getting ready to start their day. The sleeping quarters were on the top floor of one of the laundry buildings and were reported to have a "Chinesque" look about them. This reporter followed some of the Chinese men downstairs to the kitchen. Since they were using a "large hospital soup boiler" located in the yard to prepare their meals, the kitchen had become a dressing room/barbershop. When the reporter entered this room many of the Chinese men "seemed quite abashed at not being presentable ...." Continuing his tour of the living quarters used by the Chinese, the reporter entered a large sitting room that had been converted into their dining room. Here the Cantonese men were relaxing, drinking tea, or patiently waiting for their "hash" to be cooked. It did not appear they suspected their arrival would be headline news for months to come.[10]

---

[8] *Newark Evening Courier*, September 21, 1870; *Newark Daily Journal*, September 21, 1870; *Newark Daily Advertiser*, September 22, 1870; *Jersey City Evening Courier*, September 22, 1870, September 23, 1870.

[9] *Newark Daily Journal*, September 22, 1870.

[10] *Newark Daily Advertiser*, September 22, 1870.

REACTION TO THE CHINESE

The reaction of the Irish girls who would be working with the Chinese men was, for the most part, subdued. Two of the girls who had been awake when the Chinese had arrived packed their bags, collected their wages, and walked out. Others followed the next day. However, of the one hundred girls employed by Hervey less than twenty left. Moreover, many of these girls returned the day after they walked out. Some of the other girls stopped work until they were assured of their jobs.[11]

Most of the people of Belleville viewed Captain Hervey's employing Chinese labor as his own business. There was no excitement reported among the "intelligent" people of the community. The Chinese were just a good topic of conversation to these people. However, there were those who viewed the matter more seriously. A letter received by Hervey warned him that his life would be in danger unless the Chinese men were sent away by October 1. The Captain did not take this threat seriously. The Chinese began work on September 26.[12]

---

[11]*Newark Daily Journal*, September 22, 1870, reported 17 girls left, but did not mention whether any returned; *Newark Daily Advertiser*, September 22, 1870, September 28, 1870, reported 16 walked out with 12 returning; *Newark Evening Courier* September 23, 1870, reported that the girls who left would return to train the Chinese men when things were settled.

[12]*Newark Evening Courier*, September 23, 1870; *New York Herald*, September 23, 1870.

Outside of Belleville, the reaction to the new arrivals followed political party lines. The Chinese men now became the center of a political storm. A meeting of indignation was called for by one Democratic paper. Bills announcing the meeting were posted throughout Essex County. Republican papers found this call for an indignation meeting strange because the citizens of Belleville were not upset. One paper sent a reporter to investigate the matter. It was discovered that the bills calling for the meeting had been printed at the "Democratic organ" in Newark. "The whole affair" was nothing more than "an effort by the Democrats to have a little pow-wow in the suburban village." The prominent citizens of Belleville knew nothing of the call for a meeting.[13]

At seven o'clock in the evening of September 28 people began to gather in the center of Belleville for the meeting of indignation. The number of people reported to have attended the meeting varied depending on the paper. A headline of the Democratic *Newark Daily Journal* proclaimed 300 to 400 "White Working Men" had gone to Belleville to "Vigorously Protest Against Coolie Importation." The Republican *Newark Evening Courier* reported 200 spectators attended the "burlesque on an indignation meeting", most of whom were just curious. Whatever the number of spectators/participants, the tone of

---

[13]*Newark Evening Courier*, September 28, 1870.

the speakers was Sino-phobic to an extreme.[14]

The most prominent speaker was a Dr. Vail reportedly from Newark. Dr. Vail did not hesitate to use strong words or stretch the truth to suit his needs. He used a meteorological metaphor to describe the arrival of the Chinese in America. "A little cloud appeared on the horizon of California. Now it has burst here upon you." Vail went on to say Americans could never mix with the "heathen" Chinese who "will work for half price, and live upon a mouse or a rat, and call it a dainty morsel . . .." Obviously reaching for the labor vote, he continued to fabricate tales, asserting the Chinese had walked "seven miles on foot rather than pay a livery stable keeper to bring them." If America were to be saved from the heathens then the voters would have to choose the Democratic ticket in the upcoming election.[15]

After Dr. Vail spoke a Colonel Rafferty, who was running for Congress in the upcoming election, stood up to endorse all the Doctor had said. Next Michael Kenny, Counsel of the Board of Aldermen of Newark, spoke. He claimed the "Radicals intend to import thousands if not millions of these people, eventually enfranchise them and crush out the laborers with their votes." Kenny went on to describe the condition of the Chinese laborers as worse than the slaves of the

---

[14]*Newark Evening Courier*, September 29, 1870; *Newark Daily Journal*, September 29, 1870; *New York World,* September 29, 1870.

[15]*Newark Daily Advertiser*, September 29, 1870; *Newark Daily Journal*, September 29, 1870; *Newark Evening Courier*, September 29, 1870; *New York World*, September 29, 1870.

South because there were no women among them. They thus had "none of the softening influence of the other sex." Describing the shackles that were used to bind southern slaves as "mild", he then accused the Republicans of trying to "inflict on us a slavery infinitely worse" than that practiced in the South.[16]

In the Republican papers of the following day it was revealed that a letter had been sent to the chairman of the meeting. Since it was not read at the meeting, the author sent copies to the papers. In it he stated that, "Chinamen will be . . . our labor saving machines destined to perform the most laborious kinds of work . . . while our working citizens devote their time and energies to lighter work and greater gains." The *Daily Journal*, however, did not publish this letter, claiming it was "crowded out" and would be printed the next day. The letter did not appear in the following day's paper.[17]

Letters to the editor printed in the papers gave some indication of the reaction in the communities of New Jersey to the Chinese and the meeting protesting their arrival. In one letter the question of why Captain Hervey sought Chinese labor was addressed. The author stated emphatically that the reason Hervey was compelled to go to California for laborers was because of the "*unreliability*" of the

---

[16]*Newark Daily Journal*, September 19, 1870, for Rafferty running for Congress, September 29, 1870; *Newark Daily Advertiser*, September 29, 1870; *Newark Evening Courier*, September 29, 1870; *New York World*, September 29, 1870.

[17]*Newark Daily Advertiser*, September 29, 1870; *Newark Daily Journal*, September 29, 1870, September 30, 1870.

labor . . . formerly employed." He warned house servants that the "ignorance and insolence of Bridget is fast paving the way for John Chinaman to take her place in the kitchen . . .." Another letter was aimed specifically at Dr. Vail. In this letter it was revealed that Dr. Vail lived in Orange and pays his "Christian laboring man . . . one dollar less than John Chinaman receives from Mr. Hervey."[18]

Not all the letters received by the Newark papers were so supportive. One asked whether it was "a Christian principle to bring down the honest hardworking American or foreign laborer to a level with those who can . . . subsist upon starvation wages . . .. " This writer thought Chinese labor was "only one degree above slavery" and called on the people to elect officials who would pass "laws to prevent this inundation of cheap labor."[19]

The *Daily Journal* published an editorial that asked if women were not already too poorly paid. Now "this miserable Chinese element" would "supplant and deprive them of all opportunity to attain an honest living." This editorial continued in this vain while lambasting the Republicans for having allowed the importation of Chinese labor into the country "The Democrats, when they come to power will place American industry upon the high plane . . . and relieve the mechanic and working men from the necessity of

---

[18]*Newark Evening Courier*, October 1, 1870; *Newark Daily Advertiser*, October 4, 1870.

[19]*Newark Daily Advertiser*, November 30, 1870.

competing with the fifteen-cent-a-day Chinaman." Letters to the editor published in the *Journal* carried this same Sino-phobic tone. One asserted that to "vote for a Republican Congressman is to vote a contract to Koopmanchap [sic], and thus let China's pent-up millions deluge this land and drive the work men [sic] from his bench or accept a starving price for his week's labor."[20]

Articles in the Democratic press began to show an element of frustration because the working people were not upset by the arrival of the Chinese. The *Daily Journal* complained that, "No demonstration against Captain Hervey's Chow Chows and Chum Chums has been made ....." In fact, the girls at Hervey's laundry were "beginning to develop a kindly feeling towards the gentlemen of the pigtails and shaven foreheads."[21]

---

[20]*Newark Daily Journal*, September 22, 1870, September 24, 1870.

[21]*Newark Daily Journal*, September 26, 1870.

THE CHINESE AND POLITICS

With elections fast approaching the Democrats decided to make the Chinese labor issue one of their focal points during the campaign. The Democratic convention that nominated Phillip Rafferty to run in the Fourth Congressional district adopted a resolution against the importation of "coolies." This opposition to Chinese labor was not restricted to challengers. Congressman John Hill, the incumbent Republican from the Fourth Congressional district, felt obliged to inform his constituents that he opposed the importation of Chinese laborers. In a letter to the *Sussex Register* he wrote that he "looked upon this importation as another species of slavery." Congressman Orestes Cleveland, the incumbent from the Fifth Congressional district, felt it necessary to quote a speech he had made in Congress when a naturalization bill was being debated in June 1870. In this speech Cleveland stated that *"there is danger ahead from the Chinese . . ."* and that he *"would prohibit all coolies . . . ."*[22]

---

[22]*Newark Daily Journal*, September 28, 1870, October 21, 1870; *Sussex Register*, October 20, 1870. The Chinese laborers were accused of being slaves because of the way they paid for their passage to America. Their passage was paid for by labor brokers in China. The laborers then paid off the money owed for their passage from earnings in America. The Democrats claimed this was a form of slavery. They also protested that there was no labor shortage. *Newark Daily Journal*, September 29, 1870. When Swedish laborers arrived to work in Salem County, N.J. in 1873, the *Daily Journal* stated "it is hardly possible, since labor is so scarce, that any class will suffer . . ." from these new laborers. *Newark Daily Journal*, June 20, 1873. As reported in the *Daily Journal* on December 23, 1871, Miss Anna E. Dickinson, who gave a lecture for the "50th Clayton Lecture", pointed out that Wisconsin had thousands of northern Europeans who came under the same conditions as the Chinese, yet no one complained.

As the October 12 Newark charter election approached the reports or editorials of the Democratic *Daily Journal* became increasingly hysterical. Articles appeared in this paper that claimed an association using the password "Ouih" existed among the Chinese in America. It was reported that this word meant assassination and that it would be "easy . . . for the members of 'Ouih' to inaugurate an era of wholesale assassination in our midst." The small number of Chinese in the country was just the beginning. China had such a vast population that it could loss one-third of its people without notice. If America were to avoid being overrun by the Chinese the voting public would have "to vote against the party which has rendered it possible for the Chinese race to take possession of the United States and rule it in conjunction with the negros [sic]."[23]

The hysteria of the Democratic press does not seem to have impressed the voters of Newark. The Republican Party carried the October 12th election with little effort. The Republican *Evening Courier* claimed the vote was for the importation of Chinese labor. In an editorial the following day the *Journal* denounced any mechanics in Newark who had supported the Republicans. Reprinted below this editorial, after a sentence stating, "The Chinese are coming." was an advertisement from the *Daily Advertiser* offering to supply "Asiatic Laborers." The charter election was only a local election.

---

[23]*Newark Daily Journal*, October 3, 1870, October 10, 1870. "Quih" was apparently pronounced as the "qui" of quiet. The *Daily Journal* of October 3 said the Chinese were very "'Quih'-et."

Congressional elections were to be held in November, so the Democratic press continued to use the Chinese issue.[24]

In the race for the Fourth Congressional district, which included Belleville, Congressman Hill seems to have moved away from his unquestionable opposition to Chinese labor. The *Journal* reported that at a rally in Irvington Congressman Hill "tried to define his position upon the question of Chinese labor, but failed . . .."[25]

The Democrats had no doubt where the Congressman stood on this issue. The exterior of the building where the Congressman had spoken was "handsomely illuminated with Chinese lanterns, indicating a desire to extend the patronage of the party to all Chinese products." At a Republican rally a "Quartette of 'Chinese Fire-Crackers and Pop-Guns'" agreed the Chinese question would settle itself if left alone. Colonel Rafferty remained adamantly opposed to allowing the Chinese into the country. He feared that "they would rise . . . and massacre our people." The Colonel regarded "the coolie question as of immense importance" and complained that he had been condemned as a "demagogue" since the indignation meeting in Belleville. The Chinese question does not appear to have been important outside of the Belleville area. Out of the five speakers at a

---

[24] *Newark Daily Journal*, October 13, 1870.

[25] *Newark Daily Journal*, October 26, 1870.

Democratic rally held in Newark, only Congressman Cleveland mentioned the Chinese question passingly.[26]

The danger from Chinese laborers was continuously in the Democratic press in these last days before the Congressional election. A letter to the editor claimed the Chinese could not be "civilized." They have shown an "utter refusal of all overtures which seek to refine and elevate the race." This was common knowledge to anyone who had "made the history of the Chinese a careful study." The writer then went on to show his total lack of knowledge about Chinese history by claiming that from "the time of the . . . Great Wall . . . the Chinese have never tolerated the advent of missionaries among them . . .." The fact that Buddhism is an Indian religion that was spread to China by Buddhist missionaries in the second century seems to have eluded this great scholar of Chinese history.[27]

Continuing to try to use the Chinese issue, the *Daily Journal* noted the Chinese in North Adams had become skilled shoemakers in only two months. What chances were there for the youth of America to learn a trade if the Chinese proved this adept at other trades? It was then mistakenly pointed out that Massachusetts was the first state to

---

[26]*Newark Daily Journal*, October 26, 1870, October 28, 1870, November 3, 1870, November 4, 1870.

[27]*Newark Daily Journal*, October 18, 1870.

allow slavery. "Is she emulative of the distinction of being the first State to make white slavery an institution?"[28]

The *New York Evening Post* claimed that, "politics are [sic] a game which Ah Sin 'does not understand'." The *Journal* angrily replied that unscrupulous politicians could buy their votes. In this way a Presidential election could be decided "by the employment of 200,000 Chinese in the right localities . . .." The Democratic press continued to use these scare tactics; asserting Chinese labor would eventually help overturn the republic. "The process may be somewhat slow, but none the less sure." To protect America from this menace, the importation of Chinese labor had to be stopped. The Democrats were, of course, unequivocally opposed to the use or importation of Chinese labor.[29]

When the polls closed November 8th the Democrats had lost a Congressional seat in New Jersey. Republicans won both contests in the Newark-Essex County area. The vote in Belleville was 202 in favor of Congressman Hill and 159 for Colonel Rafferty. The deciding factor appears to have been the fact that Rafferty was the son of Irish-Catholic immigrants. All of the attention given to the

---

[28] *Newark Daily Journal*, October 22, 1870.

[29] *Newark Daily Journal*, November 3, 1870, quoting the *New York Post*, November 4, 1870.

question of Captain Hervey's new employees seems to have been totally ignored by the voters.[30]

As if to signal the end of the election and the return of rationalism, the *Daily Journal* printed an article on November 10th comparing America with Asia. It was stated in this article that Americans need not worry about the Chinese since American culture and Chinese culture were too different to mix. The two might eventually clash, but the stronger of the two, presumably American culture, would win. In fact, the seeds of Western culture that had already been planted in Asia would eventually take root and help Asia leave despotism behind for democratic institutions.[31]

As for the Chinese, they seemed "totally unconscious of the excitement which their presence occasioned." The atmosphere in the laundry remained peaceful. An article written by a reporter who had visited the Chinese before the indignation meeting helped dispel a few of the rumors about them that were still circulating. He reported that there was no friction between the Irish girls and the Chinese men. On the contrary, "it would be difficult to say whether they [the Chinese] were most pleased or the Irish girls who were teaching them . . . ." The new pupils quickly "attained considerable proficiency in their calling. They were quiet, industrious and contented . . . with the situation." The girls instructing the Chinese men were quickly given

---

[30]*Newark Daily Journal*, November 8, 1870, November 9, 1870.

[31]*Newark Daily Journal*, November 10, 1870.

the nickname of "Chinawomen" by the other girls the laundry. However, "all was said and accepted with the best of humour [sic]." There were no complaints heard from the girls, implying they were not displeased with the situation. One paper assured its readers this was the case because if "a woman is dissatisfied someone generally hears of it."[32]

The only problem that was reported during this early period was the difficulty of providing bath water for the Chinese. It seems they wanted to bathe twice a day. Providing the water for this proved to be a bit troublesome for Captain Hervey. The Captain did not complain because he was reaping an unexpected benefit from his new employees. The Chinese had proved to be "an immense advertisement for Captain Hervey's laundry and the town of Belleville." However, now that they were settling down to work, admittance to the laundry would be more limited. By November the novelty of the Chinese had worn off. Few people came to see them. Anyone who did come saw the Cantonese men quietly and, apparently happily working.[33]

---

[32]*Newark Evening Courier*, September 28, 1870; *New York World*, September 29, 1870.

[33]*Newark Evening Courier*, September 28, 1870, November 21, 1870.

LIFE IN THE CHINESE COLONY

After a few weeks of adjustment to their new neighbors, the citizens of Belleville began to get curious. Inevitably, questions of religion were raised. A reporter from the *Evening Courier* asked the foreman of the Chinese, Charlie Ming, about the religious beliefs of the Chinese. He told the story of three gods. One opened the sky to let in the light on chaos and created the world. A second planted the trees and crops and made the inanimate objects. The third created man. When asked where good people went after they died, Ming pointed up. As for the final destination of evil souls, he pointed down. The *Daily Journal* wryly commented that the Republican press had decided this belief was "very orthodox." If this were true then "of course the 'heathen Chinee' is all right."[34]

Needless to say, this account of Chinese beliefs did not sit well with the citizens of Belleville. Efforts were begun soon after this to bring the Christian Gospel to the Chinese. By the end of October reports about the Chinese attending services at Belleville churches began to appear in the press. In the Democratic press it was reported that seven of "Hervey's Radical Chinamen" attended services at the Belleville Dutch Reformed Church. Here they "seemed pleased with the music but when the minister gesticulated in preaching they hung their heads and laughed." Two weeks later the *Evening Courier*

---

[34]*Newark Evening Courier*, October 14, 1870; *Newark Daily Journal*, October 20, 1870.

reported thirty-two Chinese men attended services at the Episcopal Church. They "behaved with decorum and paid much attention to the services." Whether the difference in behavior between the two groups was caused by the ministers' styles or the political viewpoint of the newspapers can only be guessed.[35]

A Presbyterian missionary minister had even come to the laundry complex and offered to teach the Chinese English. In an apparent attempt to encourage the laundrymen, the minister had told them if they learned English they could move to New York and receive higher wages. This last point sent Charlie Ming to Hervey. The Chinese foreman insisted that the Minister not be allowed back into the laundry. Ming was responsible for the men fulfilling the terms of their contract. He feared the Minister would persuade some of his charges to leave before their contract expired.[36]

A New York reporter visited Belleville shortly after the Chinese attended the Episcopal service. He found the laundry complex surrounded by a fence. When he requested permission to interview the Chinese workers he was told he would have to speak with Captain Hervey. The reporter interviewed Hervey before he was given a tour of the laundry complex. Apparently annoyed by the fence, one of the first questions put to the Captain concerned its purpose. Was it

---

[35] *Newark Daily Journal*, October 31, 1870; *Newark Evening Courier*, November 14, 1870.

[36] *Newark Daily Journal*, November 17, 1870, reprinted from the *New York Sun*.

erected to keep the world out or the Chinese in? The reporter was assured that the Chinese could come and go as they wished. The fence had been constructed to keep "the rabble" out. So many people had come to see his new employees that it had become very difficult to get any meaningful work accomplished. When asked if the Chinese had come up to his expectations Hervey replied that they had not. It was not that they were idle; they just do not seem to make any "headway." The girls worked faster, but it was hoped that in a few months he might see some improvement. When asked if he had discharged any of the girls who had previously worked for him the Captain pointed out that he had actually hired a few more.[37]

The reporter then moved on to how well the Chinese were accepted in the community. As for the people of Belleville, the Captain claimed they would come to the defense of the Chinese if there were any threat of violence. The women of the laundry were getting along with their new co-workers well. In fact too well, "It is with difficulty that I keep them apart." However, Hervey did not think they would inter-marry. When the reporter asked how the Chinese spent their Sundays, he was told of their attending services in Belleville. They first attended the Dutch Reformed Church, but now attend the Episcopal Church "which services they seem to prefer." Captain Hervey then offered the reporter a tour of the facility.[38]

---

[37] *Ibid.*

[38] *Ibid.*

When he entered the laundry building, the reporter saw three groups of Chinese in three separate rooms. The Chinese were dressed in loose trousers and white over-shirts. A woman was instructing each group. After seeing the new laundrymen at work, he was introduced to Charlie Ming. Ming was asked if they were treated well and if he liked his new calling. He answered yes to both questions. What would happen if one of his men got sick or died? The foreman replied he would see to it that the body was sent back to China. Had any of his charges been sick? One member of the troop said he was sick, but Ming thought he was just lazy.[39]

Two days later Charlie Ming's opinion of his sick compatriot was proven wrong. On November 19 Ah Ling died after trouble with "dropsy". He had only worked two weeks before getting ill. Between 200 and 300 people came to watch the funeral. A local Christian minister, the Rev. Mr. Daily performed the services. The Chinese showed they were greatly affected by the loss of one of their compatriots. Before they left the grave, a bowl of rice with meat and a pair of chopsticks were placed at its head. Each of the Chinese men bowed over the grave three times to say farewell to their friend. The ladies of Belleville were kind enough to provide flowers for the funeral.[40]

---

[39] *Ibid.*

[40] *Newark Evening Courier,* November 21, 1870; *Newark Daily Advertiser,* November 22, 1870.

It was not always this peaceful within the Chinese colony in Belleville. In early 1871, one of the men wrote a friend in San Francisco to complain about the treatment received from other members of the colony. When the contents of his letter became known among the Chinese in New Jersey, the tensions that had apparently been simmering beneath the surface of the colony exploded. The Chinese fought among themselves for a half an hour. Participants reportedly used anything they could get their hands on as weapons. When the battle was over at least five of the men were so badly injured that they could not work the following day.[41]

The number of Chinese laborers employed at the laundry reached 100 by May of 1871. Captain Hervey was by then quite pleased with their performance. He was, in fact, so satisfied with his Chinese workers that he decided to increase their numbers. Charlie Ming was sent back to California in April of 1871 to speak with Ah Young about this. Any feelings of opposition to the Chinese in Belleville had by now dissipated. "Captain Hervey's 'boys'" could now walk through town "with the most perfect freedom, and are everywhere unmolested and treated with marked kindness." Coverage of this story by the Democratic press continued to be negative. After reporting the increase, an article in the *Newark Daily Journal* reported "the foreman of the laundry is now free to say that the Chinese are to

---

[41]*Newark Daily Journal*, February 2, 1871; *Newark Evening Courier*, February 2, 1871.

a great extent a failure. They learn slowly, and when they are learned [sic] they work slowly. The girls beat them all hollow."[42]

The Chinese presence in Belleville became more and more obvious as time went on. By June there were reports that the "strict rules of seclusion" at the Passaic Steam Laundry had been relaxed. "Hervey's boys" were often seen on Broad Street in Newark buying things or just window shopping.[43]

During these shopping excursions they showed a peculiar interest in weapons. One newspaper observed that, "They seem to have a *penchant* for firearms. . .." This preoccupation led to one embarrassing incident in a sporting goods store on Broad Street. A group of the Cantonese men from the Passaic Steam Laundry went to Kay's Sporting Goods in mid-1871 to purchase a pistol. After receiving instructions from Mr. Kay, one of the men fired a blank cartridge at the ceiling. When Kay turned away for a moment, his customer used his newly learned skill for one more test of the pistol he was thinking of buying. When the pistol went off it was close enough to Kay's ear to singe it. After profuse apologies, the pistol was purchased and "the Chinamen, like walking arsenals, took up their line of march for Belleville."[44]

---

[42] *Newark Daily Advertiser*, April 6, 1871, May 4, 16, 1871; *Newark Daily Journal*, April 6, 1871, May 5, 1871.

[43] *Newark Daily Journal*, June 6, 1871.

[44] *Newark Daily Journal*, June 6, 1871; *Newark Evening Courier*, June 6, 1871. Mr. Kay had a more serious incident with the guns he sold two years later when a

The Captain still insisted on certain rules being followed at the laundry. In June of 1871 some of the Chinese began gambling for pennies into the early hours of the morning. The following day they were unable to work because of a lack of sleep. Hervey insisted this practice had to stop. When he was ignored he fired two of the ringleaders and sent them back to California.[45]

Shortly after this incident 52 more Chinese laborers arrived in Belleville with the returning Charlie Ming. This brought the total of Chinese laborers employed by Hervey to 172. At least fifty Irish and American women worked with them. When questioned about not hiring more of the ladies, the Captain replied he could not find enough of them. Since the laundry had a backlog of six months' worth of work, he said he would gladly employ additional "suitable hands" if they could be found. Hervey stated he could "give employment to 100 or more girls" if he could get them. Even though he stressed that he hired the Chinese not because they were cheap, but because they were dependable, the Captain still claimed he preferred the Irish girls over the Chinese men.[46]

---

gun accidentally discharged in his store. The bullet narrowly missed him, *Newark Daily Journal*, November 14, 1873. By 1880 Kay had left the sporting goods business and was dealing in plaster balls, *Halbrook's City Directory, 1880-1881*.

[45] *Newark Evening Courier*, June 19, 1871; *Newark Daily Journal*, June 20, 1871.

[46] *Newark Evening Courier*, July 14, 1871; *Newark Daily* Advertiser, July 14, 1871, July 15, 1871; *Newark Daily Journal*, July 15, 1871.

The people of Belleville had not lost interest in the growing Chinese colony across the river. In September of 1871 a Sabbath School was founded at the Dutch Reformed Church in Belleville for the Chinese workers. The school started with fifteen students and taught English as well as the Gospel. The students were reported to be enthusiastic in their study of English and interested in the tenets of Christianity. The average number of students attending was reported to be between thirty-five and fifty.[47]

In October of 1871, members of the Belleville colony demonstrated how Americanized they had become. A group of Chinese men was returning from church when they encountered some laborers from the Midland Railroad on the Belleville Bridge. Like so many American pioneers before them, the Chinese had carried their weapons to church for protection. One of the Midland laborers, obviously not aware of the extent of the Chinese adoption of American habits, threw a rock at the Chinese. This struck one of the Cantonese men in the chest. The attack drew a quick response from the Chinese who drew their pistols and began to fire on their opponents. No one was seriously injured, but the Bergen County Sheriff arrested one of the Midland workers. In its coverage of this story, a Newark newspaper asked its readers "Who will say they are not becoming Americanized?" This adoption of American habits was

---

[47]*Newark Daily Advertiser*, August 30, 1872, September 2, 1872; *Newark Daily Journal*, December 27, 1871.

not always viewed as a positive virtue. One paper reported that the Chinese were adopting such exasperating American customs as not working one day a week and running up debts and then walking away.[48]

There was a limit to the Chinese adoption of American ways. When one of their number became ill in May of 1872, he refused to allow an American doctor to treat him. By the time a Chinese doctor could reach Belleville from New York City, all he could do was pronounce the case as hopeless. Zing Sing then asked for Charlie Ming. When Ming arrived, Zing Sing told the Chinese foreman his debts and asked that they be paid after his death.[49]

Arrangements for the funeral were "made with great pomp" because Zing Sing was so popular. 150 Chinese men dressed in their native costume and walking in pairs led the funeral procession. Following behind them were the women of the laundry, Captain Hervey and his family, and finally reporters from the newspapers. The funeral service was again conducted by the Rev. Daily.[50]

---

[48] *Newark Daily Journal*, October 23, 1871, this report claimed a Chinese man was fatally wounded by one of his comrades. Since there is no mention of a fatality in any of the other papers, I am inclined to discount this report.; *Newark Evening Courier*, October 23, 1871, this article reported only one Irish man involved. I have my doubts as to whether one man would be foolish enough to throw stones at a large group. *Newark Daily Advertiser*, September 23, 1872.

[49] *Newark Daily Advertiser*, May 15, 1872.

[50] *Ibid*, the spelling of the minister's name varies between Daily and Dally, but he is from the Methodist Church in Belleville.

Their surviving comrades visited the graves of the Chinese a few months later. Food and some whiskey were left on each grave. "The ceremony . . . was beautifully simple and eloquently brief." The occasion for this visit was a farewell party for Charlie Ming at the "village within the walls." All the Chinese had gathered outside their dormitories to say good-bye to their foreman, who was going home.[51]

The Chinese had done well while Ming had been foreman. A Chinese grocery store, which was run as a private business, was now attached to the laundry and appears to have been doing well. The Chinese laundrymen were "very diligent and careful in their work and entirely reliable." A room was set aside in the laundry complex so the Chinese could study English during their "odd hours." On one wall of the laundry a sign written in Chinese characters encouraged the workers to "Do your work well."[52]

Two months after Charlie Ming's farewell party, the *Newark Daily Journal* reported a third Chinese funeral in Belleville. Li Chow Chin, a "recently imported washman . . . fell victim to the severity of our climate." 220 Chinese men were said to have attended his funeral. A detailed description of the funeral followed. It was reported that "each (of the Chinese men) threw a piece of lighted paper upon the corpse when it was laid to rest"; that "little sticks and pieces of nickle

---

[51] *Newark Evening Courier*, August 12, 1872, this report said it was rumored Ming was going home to get married, but we know from an interview Ming gave the *Daily Journal* on September 22, 1870 that he already had a wife.

[52] *Ibid.*

[sic] currency were mingled" with the dirt covering the coffin; and that "money was distributed among the strangers" who were present. A few days after this article was printed a follow-up piece appeared. In this report it was explained that the funeral in Belleville was "more than fully reported; that is in short, no such burial took place . . .." The story was fabricated by a "penny-a-liner" and sold to the New York press.[53]

A major competitor of the Passaic Stream Laundry was the Belleville Steam Laundry across the Passaic River in Belleville. The owner of this laundry, Major William Blewett, had found it necessary to have a new building constructed in 1871. At the time Blewett had employed 70 girls and intended to increase the number to 100. The Major was not impressed with Captain Hervey's experiment. He was emphatic on this point, telling a reporter who was on hand for the opening of his new building that he "denounces Chinese help, and says that he will employ female help as long as there is a female left." However, the shortage of labor that had driven Captain Hervey to employ an increasing number of Chinese laborers was not limited to his establishment. "In the other steam laundries the distress for more female help is existing and in consequence the majority of work has to be sold without being ironed."

By November of 1872, Major Blewett had changed his mind and had about 30 Chinese men "formerly from Hervey's" working for him.

---

[53] *Newark Daily Journal*, October 18, 21, 1872.

These men must have broken their contract obligations with Captain Hervey. Ah Young did not arrive in Belleville to see about renewing the contracts of the Chinese workers until the following month.[54]

---

[54]*Newark Daily Journal*, May 5, 1871, October 24, 1871; *Newark Daily Advertiser*, May 4, 1871, November 29, 1872, December 5, 1872. In the November article it is stated that W. Blewitt had converted an old military hall for use as a laundry in Belleville. These could possibly have been converted into dormitories for his new Chinese workers.

NEWSPAPER COVERAGE

At a festival in December of 1872, Captain Hervey told his Chinese workers "it gave him great pleasure to patronize their festival, and that he was willing upon every occasion to honor their feelings as a people of a great empire." Even though the Captain was so understanding and the Chinese were accepted in Belleville, the debate over Chinese labor continued on a national scale. The reaction of America to the Chinese was at best mixed.[55]

A sarcastic editorial printed in the *New York Times* the day after Captain Hervey spoke bemoaned the civil practices of the Chinese. With biting sarcasm the *Times* informed its readers that the Chinese had nothing stronger than tea at their festival "which conclusively proved the depths of ignorance and degradation in which they are sunk." One could not blame them, however, because they were just pagans born and bred in a heathen land. It was hoped that in the future the Chinese would learn to get drunk; have free-for-alls; and knock down and trample their wives. They need only stay in a civilized country long enough. Five days later an article appeared in the same paper that was virulently Sino-phobic. The reporter wrote that he had seen "the heathens at their effeminate pursuit." He had found the Chinese working at Hervey's laundry to be too machine-like in their work. They rarely spoke and seemed "hardly aware of being

---

[55]*New York Times*, December 20, 1872. This identical article appeared in the *Newark Call* in February of the following year.

in a place called Belleville . . ..." They worked slowly but were extremely regular in their actions.[56]

When the Chinese in North Adams went on strike in August of 1873, the reaction of the *Times* was not at all hostile. Before the workers at Sampson's shoe factory struck, they "worked out faithfully the contract upon which they had entered . . .." Their conduct during the strike was "worthy of all commendation." The paper concluded Mr. Sampson did well to introduce the Chinese laborers and the Chinese do well in asking for good wages. There was obviously little editorial consistency for some newspapers when it came to the Chinese in America.[57]

This inconsistency did not extend into papers that had declared their political allegiance. The political battle that had begun with the arrival of the Chinese in 1870 continued. An example of the less than congenial editorial policies of the Democratic press toward the Chinese can be seen in the reporting of a fire at Hervey's in October of 1874. As reported in the Republican *Evening Courier*, the fire started in the drying rooms on the second floor of the largest building of the laundry. Since Captain Hervey had installed fire suppression equipment, the fire was brought under control in 30 minutes. Damage from the fire was estimated at $500.[58]

---

[56]*New York Times*, December 21, 1872, December 26, 1872.

[57]*New York Times*, August 18, 1873.

[58]*Newark Evening Courier*, October 5, 1874.

A report in the Democratic *Daily Journal* stated the "origin of the fire is a mystery, but it is supposed some vengeful Chinaman did the mischief." The report gives no source for the information about the cause of the fire. The estimated damage to the building was the same in both papers, but the Democratic paper stated that about "eighty persons, including the Chinamen, are thrown out of employment." There is no mention of a loss of jobs in the Republican press, which focused more on the state of panic the Irish women and Chinese men were in while trying to save their personal possessions. The short duration of the fire and the low estimate of damage, even in 19th century dollars brings the *Daily Journal* report into question. If one keeps in mind the Sino-phobic editorial policy of this paper, little credence can be placed in its speculation of a mischievous Chinaman.[59]

---

[59]*Newark Daily Journal*, October 5, 1874, in contrast to this report is one which appeared in the *Journal* on December 27, 1871. In this report Blewett's laundry sustained damages of $1000.00 from a fire in the upper part of the laundry. The only comment added by the paper was that insurance would cover the loss. The *Journal's* estimate for a fire in a hosiery work that was extinguished with four fire extinguishers was $400.00, *Newark Daily Journal*, May 22, 1872.

INTERACTING WITH THE OUTSIDE WORLD

It is doubtful the Chinese men at the laundry were aware of the contradictory views of the press. There were incidents in their lives, however, which made them well aware that they were not always welcome. In January of 1873 one of the members of the Belleville colony was arrested in Jersey City. Nymba Shing had followed an Irish girl who had worked at Hervey's, but was leaving for another job in New York. He had fallen in love with the girl and chose the noon train to New York to express his feelings. Apparently, he wanted to appear as Americanized as possible because he threw his arms around her while telling her how much he loved her. This type of behavior was, of course, forbidden in China where members of the opposite sex did not even hold hands in public. The girl's reaction to Nymba's expression of love was less than enthusiastic. She screamed "git out of this now, ye heathen nagur, bad luck to yees." Her shrieks produced a police officer, who arrested Nymba "on a simple charge of disorderly conduct to prevent him from following the girl to New York . . .." He was released the following day on the promise he would "return to his friends at the laundry."[60]

A few months later a French man named Thomas Edmonds saw Ah Chin and Ah Fin from Hervey's on the street in New York and decided it would be fun to pull them around by their queues.

---

[60] *Jersey City American Standard*, January 20, 1873; *Newark Daily Advertiser*, January 20, 1873.

Edmonds was arrested for assault. Since neither of the Chinese men spoke English, the Judge had to send for an interpreter from Baxter Street. After determining what had occurred, Edmonds was charged with assault, paid $300 bail, and was released. Mr. Edmonds seems to have fared better than Walter Morris. When Morris "met Ah Ping, one of Captain Hervey's heathen Chinees [sic] . . ." one Saturday night in August of 1873 he assaulted the laundry worker from Belleville. Morris spent the next ten days as a guest of the government in the county jail.[61]

Not all of the encounters the Belleville Chinese had with the police were as innocent as these. On April 4, 1874 four Chinese men from Blewett's laundry went to Newark to file a complaint with the police. They told the police they had been robbed by one of their co-workers. It was determined that the thief had left on the 7:30 train that morning. The Newark Police Chief telegraphed the Chicago Police Chief requesting the thief be arrested and detained when he arrived in Chicago. A telegram was received the following day stating the thief had been caught and was awaiting extradition. Detective P.C. Smith was sent to the windy city to pick up the culprit.[62]

---

[61]*Newark Evening Courier*, May 24, 1873; *Newark Daily Journal* August 4, 1873.

[62]*Newark Evening Courier*, April 7, 1874; *Newark Daily Journal*, April 7, 8, 10, 1874.

At 6:50 A.M. on the morning of April 11, Ah Len was brought into the First Police Precinct in Newark. The complainant is listed as Len Gun. When the defendant was brought before the judge, a clerk from Parker and Mackin's Banking House testified that Ah Len had withdrawn $645 in gold from their bank. The gold had been deposited by the prisoner in the name of Len Gun. After consideration, and the refusal of the complainant to answer his questions, the judge ruled the matter should be settled out of court. The participants in the case went to the office of Ah Len's attorney, where the matter was settled.[63]

It was not until the following year and still more trouble with the law that the newspapers got the name of the man arrested straight. Ah Len and Len Gun were one and the same person. A letter to one of the Newark papers written by the Chinese from Blewett's laundry makes this clear.[64]

The man whose money Len Gun had stolen in 1874 was actually Ah Chu. He was described by the papers as a "good-natured Chinaman." In September of 1874 Ah Chu went to the office of Judge Paulin in Newark to request a letter "certifying that he has good character and stating his troubles with Len" Gun. Chu feared Gun

---

[63]*Newark Police First Precinct Criminal Docket*, April 11, 1874; *Newark Daily Journal*, April 11, 1874; *Newark Evening Courier*, April 11, 1874.

[64]*Newark Daily Advertiser*, June 1, 1875; *Newark Evening Courier*, July 15, 16, 1874, October 27, 1874, May 27, 28, 1875; *Newark Daily Journal*, May 28, 1875. All of these articles follow the exploits of Len Gun.

would follow him to San Francisco and cause trouble there. Ah Chu was going home and wanted no trouble along the way.[65]

Ah Chu planned to spend two or three months in China and then return to Belleville. The Newark suburb seems to have been highly regarded by the Chinese. Some of the Chinese in Belleville had originally been employed in North Adams. After returning to China for a visit, they came back to America and found work in the Belleville laundries.[66]

---

[65] *Newark Evening Courier*, July 15, 16, 1874, September 5, 1874. Ah Chu's name also appears as Ah Jew. Len Gun is also spelt Len Gohn. There was really no standard form of Romanizing Chinese characters at the time.

[66] *Newark Evening Courier*, September 5, 1874; *New York Times*, June 13, 1876.

AMERICAN IGNORANCE AND OPPOSITION

Examples of pure speculation and total ignorance of Chinese customs abound in the press of the times. This ignorance began to appear in the first articles published after the arrival of the Chinese at the Passaic Steam Laundry. When a reporter saw the traditional matting used by the Chinese for sleeping he concluded the "new laundrymen had showed their disgust for Americanisms by putting pieces of matting on top of the carefully made up white folks beds."[67]

These beds appear to have been of a sturdy iron construction, much as one might expect in an industrial dormitory setting and were, of course, provided by Captain Hervey. Yet, after viewing the sleeping arrangements provided to the Chinese this reporter wrote that "Chinamen become so fascinated by the berths on the vessels which bear them from their native land that anything in the shape of a berth seems ever after to them the perfection of sleeping places." This reporter's suppositions concerning the sleeping habits of the Chinese were rather innocent. More malicious were the charges of the Chinese feasting on the neighborhood vermin that appeared in the press throughout this period.[68]

---

[67] *Newark Daily Advertiser*, September 22, 1870.

[68] *Ibid*. References to the Chinese eating rats appeared in the *Newark Daily Journal*, September 27, 28, 1870, December 1, 1870, September 10, 1875; *Newark Evening Courier,* September 29, 1870, August 12, 1872; *Newark Daily Advertiser*, December 19, 1870.

One of the more humorous observations that appeared in the Newark papers of the times concerned a Buddhist monk visiting New York City. After reporting that Chow Ju Tren came to America every ten years, no small feat since he was in his eighties, the paper described him as being "very bald." Since all who enter the Buddhist clergy have their heads shaved, this should not have been surprising. Chow's age may have been why the reporter felt it necessary to point this out. However, if an inquiry had been made the reporter would have discovered the Buddhist practice and been able to tell his readers a little more about China. Although the reporter's observation was accurate, his lack of an explanation as to why the monk was bald implies it was less than astute.[69]

There appears to have been no effort on the part of the American press to educate its readers on Chinese history or customs. In a report on the origin of the celebration of the Chinese Lunar New Year, the *New York Times* gave credit for the beginning of the holiday to an Emperor Ju, who started the "present dynasty" 5000 years before. The "present dynasty" was the Ch'ing Dynasty which was founded in 1644.[70]

Politicians shared this confusion about the dynasty then ruling China. One Democratic nominee for Congress in Ohio, claimed the Chinese had been "ruled for the past six hundred years by a little band

---

[69]*Newark Evening News*, September 13, 1886.

[70]*New York Times*, February 13, 1888.

of Tartars, who, under the leadership of Ghengis Khan, overrun [sic] and conquered that vast and populous empire." Ghengis Khan had only conquered northern China and was a Mongol not a Tartar. It was left to his grandson Kubilai to finally overthrow the Southern Song dynasty in 1279. However, the Mongols were driven back to the Asian steppes by the Chinese in 1368. [71]

In an article printed in the *Newark Evening News*, a man formerly from California claimed that all of the Chinese in America were owned by one of six trading companies, with an astronomical capital base of $140,000,000. He assured the reporter that after a laborer had earned $300 he had to return to China. If any laborer broke his contract with these companies he was killed by a gang called the "highbinders." This former Californian also asserted that everything purchased by the Chinese in America had to be obtained through the six companies. Continuing to paint as dark and inaccurate a picture as possible, he stated that there were no Chinese women east of the Rockies because the climate was too cold. He then went on to seemingly contradict himself by saying that Chinese women were brought and sold as slaves. Obviously, the power of these slaves over their masters was so great that they could dictate where they would live.[72]

---

[71] *Newark Daily Journal,* October 8, 1870.

[72] *Newark Evening News,* December 10, 1886.

Occasionally, an accurate account of Chinese customs did appear in the newspapers. In one article the reason Chinese laundry signs were usually painted red was explained. A Secretary of the Chinese Legation in Washington, D.C. had explained that "as a rule . . . the laundrymen are not the most educated men in the Flowery Kingdom, and are somewhat inclined to be superstitious. In China the color red is considered very lucky, and for that reason the laundrymen have their signs painted that color."[73]

---

[73] *Newark Evening News*, July 17, 1886. The Six Companies were benevolent organizations that were organized based on districts in Canton province and dialects spoken. They provided social services for members. See Iris Chang's The Chinese in America, pages 78 - 80.

THE LUNAR NEW YEAR

It was in reports about the Lunar New Year that the press put its greatest effort into accurately portraying the Chinese. This was the time of year when Belleville was transformed into microcosm of Chinese culture. In late January or early February reports of how the Chinese celebrated their New Year in Belleville often appeared in the press.

The Chinese New Year was first celebrated in Belleville in 1871. The population of the Chinese colony was 81. Two of these worked as cooks; two were laborers; while the rest ironed. On a sometimes rainy February weekend these men introduced the people of Belleville to the festivities of the Chinese New Year. Work stopped at the laundry at noon Friday the 17th and did not begin again until the morning of the 21st. On Saturday "free and easy" ceremonies commemorating the ancestors of the laundrymen were held.[74]

The rest of Saturday was spent observing the Chinese custom of visiting one's friends at New Year. Members of the Belleville colony visited "each other in their twenty rooms . . . treating one another to candies and Chinese preserves." On Sunday "they had a big dinner and a jolly time generally." The day was celebrated with "music, feasting and other demonstrations delightful to the peculiar people."

---

[74] *Newark Daily Advertiser*, February 17, 1871; *Newark Daily Journal*, February 18, 1871, February 20, 1871; *Newark Evening Courier*, February 20, 1871.

A group of the Chinese men visited Newark on Monday morning and "were highly delighted with the show windows and neatly painted signboards along Broad street [sic]." The celebration ended that night "with a grand display of Chinese pyrotechnics."[75]

It was not until February of 1875 that reports of the Lunar New Year celebration in Belleville appeared again. By that time the festivities had grown considerably, but the time the Chinese spent away from work had declined. Prior to this year the Cantonese men had taken an entire week to celebrate. The 1875 observance lasted only three days. The reason less time was spent celebrating this year was economics. Previously, the Chinese had been paid a monthly salary, so "no reduction of wages was made on account of idleness." Now they were paid by the piece. Time away from work cost them money.[76]

The brevity of the holiday did not dampen the spirits of the nearly 100 Chinese in Belleville. The colony at Captain Hervey's Passaic Steam Laundry had "made preparations to outrival all previous celebrations of the kind in this country." They had the advantage of being in a country setting. Unlike the cramped quarters reported at Baxter Street in New York the previous year, the Chinese in Belleville had a large courtyard and a large dormitory building to use

---

[75]*Newark Evening Courier*, February 18, 1871; *Newark Daily Journal*, February 20, 1871.

[76] *Paterson Daily Press*, February 6, 1875; *Newark Daily Journal*, February 8, 1875; *Newark Evening Courier*, February 8, 1875.

for their celebration   They had also ordered supplies from China to enliven the festivities. A reported 100,000 firecrackers were set off. The fireworks display so impressed one reporter that he was forced to conclude Americans had a lot to learn from the Chinese about firecrackers. The celebration was attended by 300 people. Those in attendance included Chinese from throughout northern New Jersey as well as the American friends of the Chinese.[77]

Another factor drawing the Chinese to Belleville was a "Joss" temple that was located on the second floor of the Chinese dormitory. If the description of this temple is compared to that of other temples located in New York and San Francisco, the Belleville temple would be the largest of its kind in America. Since many of the Chinese felt worship at a temple was required for an auspicious start to the New Year, a visit to the temple at Belleville was no small matter.[78]

Even after Captain Hervey sold the Passaic Steam Laundry in August of 1875, the New Year celebrations continued. The purchaser of the laundry was a George Casebolt. Born in what was to become West Virginia, Casebolt had been a businessman in San Francisco. He was frequently in Newark purchasing supplies for his carriage

---

[77] *New York Times,* February 16, 1874; *New York Tribune,* August 21, 1875, September 6, 1875.

[78] *New York Tribune,* August 21, 1875, September 6, 1875; *New York Times,* February 16, 1874.

hardware factory. Prior to becoming a partner in the laundry, Casebolt had apparently owned some shares of the enterprise He continued Captain Hervey's tolerant policy toward the Chinese. The Chinese New Year celebration of 1877 went off much as in preceding years. The fireworks display was also equal to the years before.[79]

The size of the colony at Casebolt's laundry had declined to ninety-eight by mid-1880. They were a young group; the majority of them were under thirty. Very few reports were published on what their daily life consisted of. A limited picture, however, can be drawn from these few articles.[80]

---

[79]*Newark Daily Advertiser*, February 13, 1877; *Newark Daily Journal*, February 14, 1877. The laundry was sold to George Casebolt on August 4, 1875, see deed at Bergen County, N.J. Clerk's Office Book O-9, Page 39; *Newark Call*, October 9, 1932, in an interview the 93 year old Casebolt made some absurd claims. Most of what he said I have discounted considerably. I take him at his word only for his place of birth, what he did prior to becoming heavily involved in the laundry, and the possibility he had purchased shares in the business while still living in San Francisco. Captain Hervey apparently remained in the area, but became known as "Esquire." He read the Declaration of Independence for the July 4th celebration of 1876; *Newark Daily Journal*, July 5, 1876.

According to an essay in the Belleville Federal Writer's Project, Captain Hervey was supposed to have declared his use of Chinese labor a failure in 1873. The paper cited for this pronouncement was the *Princeton Press*. I have been unable to locate a copy of this paper, but doubt the accuracy of this information. The Newark press did not carry this story. Princeton seems to be a little too distant from Belleville to have firsthand information about events at the Passaic Steam Laundry. Since there are so many inaccuracies in this essay, I have chosen to ignore this claim, as well as most of the other information contained in this Sino phobic piece.

[80] *Newark Daily Advertiser*, February 4, 1881, February 18, 1882, February 7, 1883, February 8, 1883; *New York Times*, February 19, 1882, February 7, 1883, February 8, 1883, January 28, 1884; *Newark Evening News*, January 28, 1884. *United States Census, 1880*, Rutherford, Union Township, Bergen County, New Jersey.

As with their compatriots throughout the New York-New Jersey area, the daily life of the Chinese employed at Casebolt's was made up of work. It was reported that they stopped work for only ten minutes each day in order to eat lunch. Then they would go back to their ironing boards. At six o'clock they would end their day and eat dinner. The evening hours were used to relax and by nine thirty they were in bed. True to the purpose of many of the Cantonese men who came to America, they labored and saved for the future. Stories of their frugality began to appear as early as 1875.[81]

The one time of the year when all of this was put aside was the Chinese Lunar New Year. The New Year celebration of the Chinese colony had grown considerably since the people of Belleville were first introduced to the festival. Although there were occasional additions to the celebration, for the most part the men from Canton followed the traditions they had learned as youngsters. Their celebration drew Chinese from all over the New York-New Jersey area. Much to the chagrin of its Chinese inhabitants, New York City still would not allow the Chinese to celebrate their festival on the streets of the city. With no other option, the Chinese from that city traveled to Belleville. "It was known to all Chinamen in New York and in the neighboring cities and towns that the grand effort to rid

---

[81] *Newark Daily Advertiser*, June 9, 1875; *Newark Daily Journal*, June 9, 1875; *New York Times*, December 26, 1872, February 19, 1882.

their race of the Evil One in the time-honored manner of the New Year's festivities was to be made at Belleville . . . ."[82]

Some of the New York Chinese would travel in grand style by coach to the New Jersey suburb, smoking cigars and drinking liquor to pass the time. Train seems to have been the more common means of reaching the laundry across the river from the suburban village.[83]

It was not an inexpensive celebration. The estimated total cost for the 1882 celebration was $1500. The cost of the fireworks alone was $500. This may have been an exceptionally costly year because the Joss Temple had been "refitted." 500 people took part in that year's festivities. Chinese from Newark and Paterson joined the New Yorkers who converged on Belleville. Many of these guests were accompanied by their Irish wives. The dinner "overshadowed anything of the kind ever set before their guests in other years" and consisted of chicken, pork, and sweetmeats.[84]

By now the colony in Belleville was so firmly entrenched that it could support two stores where "tea and other articles" could be purchased. Although the celebration remained shorter than the fifteen days traditionally set aside in China, the Cantonese men made the

---

[82] *Newark Daily Advertiser*, February 4, 1881; *New York Times*, February 19, 1882.

[83] *New York Times*, February 19, 1882.

[84] *Paterson Daily Press*, February 6, 1875; *New York Times*, February 19, 1882.

most of the time they had. Apparently the Americans were enjoying the Lunar New Year as much as the Chinese. Some citizens of Belleville made the trip across the Passaic River to view the celebration.[85]

The number of Chinese men employed at the Passaic Laundry was reported to have dropped to seventy-five by the Lunar New Year of 1882. The following year the number of Chinese employed at Casebolt's actually increased to eighty-five. In February of that year a reporter visited a neighborhood laundry on Bank Street in Newark to inquire about the New Year celebration. The establishment was owned by Sam Sing. Sing, who was looked upon as a leader by the Chinese of that city, suggested the reporter "go to Belleville, have most fun there." The following day, this reporter took Sing's advice and went to the suburban village where he was courteously received by Casebolt . . . ."[86]

The celebration in Belleville continued to draw Chinese from around the New York-New Jersey area. It was acknowledged by the

---

[85] *Newark Daily Advertiser*, February 4, 1881; *New York Times*, February 19, 1882. It was pointed out in this article that there had never been a marriage between Chinese and Irish workers at the laundry. This implies that the experience of Nymba Shing nine years before had not been forgotten. The reported length of the New Year celebration varied with each paper. The *New York Times* reported the festival lasted a week. The *Daily Journal* claimed that the celebration was reduced from a week to three days because the men changed from salaried employees to paid-by-the-piece workers, *Newark Daily Journal*, February 5, 1875.

[86] *New York Times*, February 19, 1882; *Newark Daily Journal*, February 5, 1875.

press that, "nowhere is the festival observed with more éclat than among the Chinamen employed at Casebolt's on the opposite side of the river from Belleville." The Joss house remained the only one of its kind in the area. Chinese from New York City continued to make the trip to New Jersey where they would "unite with the Chinamen there in religious observations . . . ."[87]

By the Lunar New Year of 1884, the Chinese employees of the Passaic Steam Laundry reportedly numbered ninety, with more being hired when needed. A reporter traveling on a Belleville street car witnessed a disagreement between two Chinese men that brought into focus the Chinese custom of paying off one's debts at the New Year. One of the Cantonese men was insisting he owed the other thirty cents. This was denied by his companion and the thirty cents was placed on the seat between them, both refusing to take the money.[88]

When the men arrived at the laundry complex there were already 100 people in the courtyard. The sound of small caliber firearms and firecrackers filled the air and what appears to have been a Ch'ing

---

[87] *Newark Daily Advertiser*, February 7, 8, 1883; *New York Times*, February 7, 8, 1883.

[88] *Newark Evening News*, January 28, 1884. In this article and in all subsequent stories the *Evening News* claims that the leader of the Chinese colony is Charlie Ming. The only other paper to place Ming in Belleville after his reported departure in 1872 was the *New York Times* in an article in December of 1884. In this piece the *Times* explained that Ming had returned to China earlier that year because of failing health. I am inclined to believe Ming probably returned to China in 1872 since several papers mention other men performing his supposed duties as interpreter.

Dynasty flag with a dragon on a yellow background was flying from the flagpole. New Yorkers continued to make the trek across the Hudson with almost "half the Chinese residents of the City (celebrating in) Belleville . . . where the only Joss House in this country is situated . . .." Compared to the New Jersey celebration, the festivities in New York City were dreary. These consisted of a few firecrackers being set off in the rear of tenements and tom-tom drums sounding in the basements of these buildings in the evening. At Casebolt's, dinner was served at three o'clock when "all of the five hundred Chinamen present partook freely."[89]

In February of 1885 the *New York Times* reported, Chinese "from all parts of . . . [New York] State were due in Belleville . . . at as early an hour as trains and other travel would permit." The number of colony members had declined to 60. These men were "considered as a happy nucleus of Chinese society . . . Belleville itself was described as "all . . . life and bustle and Chinamen." The people of the suburban village wished the Chinese a happy New Year as they passed on the street. The reporter from the *Times* implied that there was some resentment toward the Cantonese men among some of the townspeople. However, he gave no evidence to support this supposition. The celebration of this year was special because it was a year set aside for the forgiveness of one's sins. When speculating on what sins the Chinese had committed this reporter concluded that,

---

[89] *Ibid*; *New York Times*, January 28, 1884.

"terrible injuries to unoffending shirt bosoms doubtlessly form the background of John Chinaman's sins."[90]

After the New Year's celebration ended the Chinese resumed "work at the ironing boards and wash tubs for another year." This was the last year the Lunar New Year celebration in Belleville was reported in the press. In December of 1886 the Belleville colony was dispersed because of pressure from organized labor.[91]

---

[90] *New York Times*, February 16, 1885.

[91] *Newark Evening News*, February 16, 1885.

CHINESE EXCLUSION

While the Chinese at Casebolt's enjoyed their Lunar New Year celebrations, events occurred on the national level that would limit the number of Chinese workers available for these festivals. The Sinophobic exclusion movement had been gaining momentum nationally since the late 1870s. In February of 1879 Congress passed a bill that prohibited any ship from carrying more than fifteen Chinese passengers to an American port. President Hayes vetoed this bill. The reasoning behind his veto was not the President's sense of fair play. The problem Hayes had with this bill was that it violated American treaty obligations.[92]

According to the Burlingame Treaty signed by the United States and China in 1868, immigration between the two countries could not be restricted. Realizing the mood of the country and agreeing that some restriction of Chinese immigration was desirable, Hayes sent a diplomatic mission to China to obtain the right to limit the number of Chinese coming to America. On November 17, 1880 the Angell Treaty, which allowed the United States to suspend Chinese immigration for a "reasonable" time, was signed. Laborers were the only group of Chinese supposedly affected by these restrictions, "other classes not being included in the limitation." On May 6, 1882

---

[92]Alexander DeConde, *A History of American Foreign Policy*, Third Edition (New York: Charles Scribner's Sons, 1978), Volume I: Growth to World Power (1700-1914), pg. 275.

President Chester Arthur signed the first Chinese Exclusion law. This law prohibited entrance into the United States by Chinese laborers for ten years.[93]

The people of Belleville do not appear to have paid much attention to the Sino-phobic cries that made passage of this legislation popular. In fact one article published in 1885 stated that the "Belleville people relate with pride how the Chinese are not afraid to stay among them, and how the first Chinese colony ever settled in the Eastern states - at North Adams, Mass. - proved a failure because the North Adamites didn't know how to handle it." Many of the people of the New Jersey suburb had put effort into getting to know the Chinese employed at the laundries in the area. The efforts of the Sabbath School that was founded in 1871 for the Chinese finally came to fruition in 1882. In that year thirty-five of the Chinese men in the area became members of the Dutch Reform Church in Belleville.[94]

Life for members of the Belleville colony does not seem to have been effected by the passage of the Exclusion Act.

---

[93] *Ibid.* The 1882 Exclusion Act was not the first restrictive immigration law enacted. The Page Act of 1875 forbad the entry of Asian women who are or might become prostitutes. This effectively closed America to Asian women because all could potentially become prostitutes. Prostitution was a common occupation among the few Chinese women in the US at the time.

[94] *New York Times*, February 16, 1885; *The history of the Old Church in the Valley: The 275th Anniversary of the Belleville Dutch Reformed Church*, Privately Printed, 1979.

CONTINUING AMERICANIZATION

Even though the Cantonese men held onto their traditions for their Lunar New Year celebration, they continued to adopt certain American customs. One of these was the work stoppage. Following the example set by their countrymen in North Adams earlier, the Belleville Chinese struck for higher wages. Their main complaint appears to have been they were not paid by the piece, but were under contract that paid them a salary. The ironers must have realized that if they were paid at a piece rate they could more easily increase their wages by working harder. Since the other workers of the laundry had been paid by the piece since 1870, the Chinese may have also viewed the issue as one of equal treatment. Even when they struck there was little trouble between them and Mr. Casebolt, who explained that when "they strike they go home and wait for me to come to terms."[95]

In December of 1884 the Chinese struck for a different reason. In this instance the striking workers were also more violent than they had previously been. The trouble came about after Casebolt had decided to break his ironers of a bad habit. It seems the Chinese men "had a habit, if a shirt has been imperfectly ironed, of crumbling it up, so that it must be washed [again] . . .." In order to put an end to this,

---

[95]*Newark Daily Journal*, September 22, 1870; *New York Times*, February 16, 1885; *Newark Evening News*, December 15, 1886. The first report of the Cantonese men being paid by the piece appeared in the *Newark Daily Journal*, February 5, 1875.

an "order was lately issued that any Chinaman who indulged in this nefarious practice would be discharged."[96]

On December 16th one of the Chinese ironers, Ah Fee, crumbled up a shirt and threw it back to be re-washed. The superintendent of the laundry, George W. Cummings, saw Ah Fee's frustrated reaction and promptly fired him. Ah Fee informed Quong Long, the interpreter for the colony, who then told their Chinese co-workers. Upon hearing of Ah Fee's dismissal, the men in the ironing room refused to work until their compatriot was re-hired. Cummings' action was appealed to Casebolt. After hearing that Casebolt had upheld his superintendent's decision the Chinese walked out.[97]

The Cantonese men "went to their quarters and held a council of war. A few moments later they issued forth armed with hammers, tongs, long-handled saucepans, and other war-like instruments." The angry ironers ran into the main laundry building. Mr. Cummings, seeing the trouble coming and deciding discretion was the better part of valor, fled out another door. The superintendent sought refuge in the neighboring Jersey City Water Power Works where George Beatty, a former Newark policeman, was the watchman. Beatty came to Cummings' aid when he saw the latter run onto the Water Works property. Wearing an old police jacket and carrying a police club, the former officer of the peace "awed the innocent Celestials," who beat a

---

[96] *Newark Daily Advertiser*, December 18, 1884.

[97] *Newark Evening News*, December 17, 18, 1884.

hasty retreat. After a short while the Chinese settled down and made their way back to their quarters.[98]

The attack on Cummings hardened Casebolt's attitude. When the situation was calm enough for mediation, the Chinese men were given a choice. In addition to the dismissal of Ah Fee, they would have to accept the firing of four others who were judged to be the ringleaders of their small uprising. If they would not accept these terms "the whole colony of Chinese would have to get out of their quarters. This is the greatest trouble they have, as in that case their Eastern headquarters would be broken up. In the second story of the building . . . is the only 'joss' house in the East . . .." Possibly because the decision to be made would affect more than just the fifty to sixty Cantonese men still employed at the Passaic Steam Laundry, a meeting concerning the matter was held on Mott Street in New York City.[99]

Meanwhile, rumors of violence at the laundry spread quickly. It was generally believed in Newark that the Chinese had assassinated Casebolt. "The greatest consternation prevailed in Belleville as people from the surrounding communities went to the village to find

---

[98]*Newark Evening News*, December 17, 1884; *New York Times*, December 18, 1884.

[99]*Newark Evening News*, December 18, 1884; *Newark Morning Register*, December 19, 1884. It is possible the Chinese men held their meeting at 16 Mott Street which was called the Chinese City Hall of New York in the *New York Times* on December 8, 1884.

out the truth. The number of curiosity seekers grew so great that police were called in for crowd control.[100]

Casebolt began to talk to reporters about the happenings at the laundry. He claimed to be amused by the reports of his assassination. The reporter was informed by Casebolt that the "Chinese in this country are a harmless lot of creatures." However much faith the owner of the laundry had in this statement, a policeman was still stationed in his office during this interview. Casebolt then went on to explain that it was "a popular error, that Chinese labor is cheap. Such is not the case. They make very good workmen, but they cost more than white labor." Obviously he was willing to pay for his premium labor and his ironers were reluctant to leave the laundry so the crisis passed. It did not leave the colony unscathed. The New Jersey State census taken in mid-1885 showed the number of Chinese staying in the dorms at Casebolt's had dropped to thirty-six.[101]

By the time of the Lunar New Year celebration of 1885, Casebolt had forgotten the trouble of December. When speaking with a *New York Times* reporter, the owner of the Passaic Steam Laundry described the Chinese as "good fellows, and a much maligned class . . . .They're good men and that's the long and the short of it."

---

[100] *Newark Morning Register*, December 18, 1884.

[101] *Ibid. New Jersey State Census 1885*, Bergen County, Union Township, Rutherford. These numbers reflected only those who resided in the dorms of the laundry. It is possible that a small number did not stay there.

He continued to allow the Cantonese men to celebrate the Lunar New Year on the property of the laundry.[102]

There was little reported on the Belleville colony until May, when the Christians among the Cantonese men hosted an "entertainment" at the Sabbath school. Ten Lung led the group, who sang hymns and recited the Ten Commandments. The Rev. Mr. Brokaw then addressed the gathering and used the opportunity to rebuke those who did not accept the Chinese. After the Reverend had finished, Ten Lung stood up to express the thanks felt by the Chinese. He described how the Cantonese men had arrived in Belleville strangers, of their feeling lonely, and of the help given by the Sabbath school with both the English language and Christianity. Afterwards, all were invited to dinner. Music for the occasion was provided by a Chinese theater band from New York City.[103]

---

[102] *New York Times*, February 16, 1885; *Newark Evening News*, February 16, 1885.

[103] *Sentinel of Freedom*, May 26, 1885.

THE END OF THE FIRST CHINESE COMMUNITY

In December of 1886 the Sino-phobic forces that had until then been resisted by the people of Belleville finally brought an end to the first Chinese colony in New Jersey. On December 11th the Executive Board of District 51 of the Knights of Labor reached an agreement with George Casebolt. Casebolt agreed to discharge the thirty or so Chinese laborers still in his employ if the Knights of Labor supplied competent help. The white employees of the Passaic Steam Laundry had complained about working with the Chinese. "American hands said they could no longer stand the habits and customs of the Celestials, and, besides, they felt it an outrage on American labor to keep them on the same industrial plane with American working people."[104]

If Casebolt had not agreed to the Knights demands, the union had threatened to call for a strike. Casebolt's explanation for retaining Chinese labor for so long "was . . .[that] competent white labor was hard to procure." Since the Knights of Labor had promised to supply him with the competent help he needed, the laundry owner was willing to let the Chinese go.[105]

---

[104] *Newark Evening News*, December 11, 1886; *The Sentinel of Freedom*, December 14, 1886.

[105] *Newark Evening News*, December 15, 1886.

The Chinese men were told of the decision on the afternoon of December 14th. The remaining members of the Belleville colony held a conference that night. Their reaction to Casebolt's decision was subdued. The following morning a truck was hired to transport their property.[106]

The Chinese laborers leaving was "quite an event for Belleville. . . ." Contrary to many of the articles written over the sixteen years the Chinese were in that community, one paper reported that the people of the village never "looked upon them with favor . . . ." In this same article, however, it was stated that some of the Cantonese men spent the morning of the 15th making presents for their American friends. By December 16th the Chinese had left Belleville.[107]

The destination of those Chinese interviewed by the newspapers was New York City. One planned to open a grocery store in that city. Another went to join his cousin in Brooklyn.[108]

Chinese from Belleville had actually been leaving the Passaic Steam Laundry and striking out on their own for more than a decade when George Casebolt released the last of his Chinese employees. As the term of their contracts ran out many of the Cantonese men left the laundry across the river from Belleville to start their own businesses. Some of these men appear to have moved to the surrounding

---

[106]*Ibid.*

[107]*Ibid.*

[108]*Ibid.*

communities, others were drawn to the large metropolis across the Hudson River east of the suburban village. The enterprises they started included selling cigars or candy, but the "goodly portion invested their earnings in little wash shops."[109]

---

[109] *Ibid; Newark Daily Journal,* September 10, 1875.

BECOMING PART OF AMERICA

"Hervey could not have foreseen that his decision would plant the seeds of future Chinatowns along the East Coast. Many of his former employees moved to New York City or Newark, New Jersey and from there wrote their relatives, inviting them to join them in opening laundries of their own."[110] In 1870 there were thirty-eight people in New Jersey who were born in China. New York City had a small enclave of Chinese, most of whom were sailors or worked making cigars. There were no Chinese laundries in the area.

Neighborhood Chinese laundries began to appear in Newark by mid-1873. In August of that year it was reported that "Not many months ago" a Chinese laundry was opened on "Broad street [sic], near Bridge." Business was apparently good "for soon afterwards another similar firm . . . commenced in an adjoining basement." A third was located "just below the North Reform Church." The fourth of these establishments opened in mid-August. The "lordly and unctuous proprietor being an individual calling himself Ya Youn. Ya Youn is a man of great energy, and with the assistance of several Chinese is bound to draw custom and make his business a success."[111]

---

[110] Iris Chang, *The Chinese in America*, (New York, Viking Press, 2003), p. 102. The *New York Tribune* reported in 1885 that a brother of one of the Passaic Steam Laundry workers had opened a laundry at Catherine St. & East Broadway in New York City. *New York Tribune,* June 21, 1885.

[111]*Newark Daily Journal*, August 15, 1873; *Newark Daily Advertiser*, August 16, 1873; *Newark Evening Courier*, August 16, 1873.

Laundries were ideal for any Chinese man who had the spirit of an entrepreneur. Little English was required to run such an enterprise; startup costs were minimal; and there was a growing need for this type of service. In 1875 there were only five laundries listed in a Newark City Directory. It should be pointed out that none of these was Chinese owned, so this figure is obviously inaccurate. However, there can be little doubt that there were a limited number of laundries in Newark at the time.[112]

The number of laundries increased dramatically over the next decade. By 1886 there were forty-six Chinese laundries listed in the Directory. The only competition faced by the Chinese men was from six steam laundries. By this time the Chinese had acquired a reputation for being "unsurpassed" in "laundry work." The Chinese laundry men did not go unopposed. There were periodic attempts at organizing non-Chinese steam laundries in Newark "to fight the Chinese." In December of 1886, the *Newark Evening News* reported that "The anti-Chinese laundry movement in this city has at last taken definite shape." The justification for organizing was that the prices Chinese laundries charged were "made possible by their habits of life and employment of cheap labor." Two young men who had started a laundry brought the complaint before the Central Orange Labor Union. In a letter to the union, they stated that the Chinese laundries "were

---

[112]*Holbrook's City Directory*, Newark, N.J.-1875, Business Section, Holbrook City Directories, Inc., Newark, N.J.

supported, not as popularly supposed by dudes, but by working men." The letter asked the union to tell its members not to patronize the Chinese. A resolution was passed for the union president to appoint a committee to track members going into Chinese laundries. A similar movement was started in 1890 with the stated goal of "removing every laundry operated by the Mongolians in New York, Brooklyn, and New Jersey." 1898 saw another attempt to drive the Chinese from the market. The Women's League of New York called for a boycott of Chinese laundries, stating they would have women "detectives" keeping an eye on laundries to report union people patronizing them. These campaigns do not appear to have affected the Chinese laundry men in New Jersey.[113]

1895 saw the number of laundries in Newark increase to eighty-five. The first Chinese restaurant and Chinese grocery store had appeared on Fair Street. Within ten years Newark's Chinatown was firmly established, anchored by restaurants and grocery stores along the former Fair Street, now named Lafayette Street. This section of Lafayette Street remained "the stronghold of the resident Chinese" until after 1907. In 1910 there were ten Chinese restaurants in the city. These had moved away from Lafayette Street with six on Market

---

[113] For Evidence on the growth in the number of laundries during this period see: *Holbrook's City Directory, Newark, New Jersey*, Holbrook City Directories, Inc., Newark, New Jersey, 1875-1886. *Holbrook's City Directory*, Newark N.J. 1886-1887; *Newark Evening News*, November 2, 1886, December 28, 1886; *Newark Daily Advertiser,* December 28, 1886, January 25, 1887; *New York Times*, March 21, 1890; *New York Tribune*, January 23, 1898..

Street and one each on Broad, Mulberry, Mechanic, and Orange Streets. That year also saw the construction of what became known as the Mulberry Arcade which ran along an alley between Green and Lafayette Streets and would "serve as a center of Chinese commercial and community life . . ." for the next few decades.[114]

The two buildings of the Arcade had stores running along their first floor with apartments above for the proprietors of these establishments. Along with the small businesses run by these men during the day, a lucrative gambling trade grew and Chinatown grew with it. The winnings were said to have been shared generously at the local restaurants. Men came from New York on the Hudson Tubes to enjoy themselves.[115] Opium dens were also located in this "mysterious" district running behind Newark's City Hall. Newark's Chinatown reached its height in the late 1920's and early 1930's.

All of this activity drew the attention of the Newark Police who conducted frequents raids. February 5, 1928 saw a drug raid of the area with $1,500 worth of opium seized. On June 20, 1930, police raided Mulberry Street, arresting 73 and confiscated $15,000 worth of drugs and paraphernalia.[116] The narcotics raids continued. On

---

[114] *Newark Evening News*, February 12, 1907; *The Newark Star Ledger* October 14, 1956.

[115] A bartender living in the Arcade in 1958 claimed that "during the early years of the depression waitresses in one Mulberry St. restaurant added $100 tips to their $10 weekly salaries." *Newark Evening News,* June 8, 1958.

[116] *Newark Evening News,* February 5, 1928, June 21, 1930, June 8, 1958.

February 2, 1931, fifty Federal narcotic agents raided Chinatown, arresting 163, destroying 16 opium dens, and confiscating nearly $5,000. It should be pointed out that only 18 of the 163 men were charged with any crime.[117]

As with all illegal activity, the gambling and opium attracted organized crime. In the Chinese community this meant the Hip Sing and On Leung tongs. The press reported that members of the Hip Sing tong were for the most part laundry men. While the On Leong membership was for the most part made up of business and restaurant owners.[118] These two factions went to war in 1905, 1924, and 1927. In August of 1905, the two factions battled it out in a theater in New York City. The "architect of the affair" was said to be Mock Duck, the leader of the Hip Sing tong. He placed his men in the front and the rear of the theater. On Leong men were in the center. When fireworks were set off, the Hip Sing men began to shoot. Four were killed with many others injured. The cause was said to be gambling, with On Leong men testifying in court against Mock Duck and Hip Sing members. An editorial in the *New York Times,* warned the Chinese to police themselves or Americans would be more inclined to restrict them.[119]

---

[117] *Newark Evening News,* February 2, 1931, February 17, 1931.

[118] *Newark Evening News,* March 24, 1927.

[119] *New York Times*, August 7, 1905, August 8, 1905.

In October of 1924, the body of a Chinese man was found in North Arlington on Schuyler Avenue. It was the second murder of a Chinese man in the New York/New Jersey area in a week and was thought by the authorities to be part a tong war.[120] Newark's response was an increased police presence along Mulberry Street to prevent any further violence. Police seized papers that included a list of Hip Sing members with their names, addresses, and phone numbers. Newark was now assumed to be Hip Sing headquarters. Groups of Chinese gathered in the street and then quickly dispersed. All the while a crowd of non-Chinese stood across from the Mulberry Arcade to watch the happenings. A two year truce was finally signed on March 24, 1925 after 72 people had been killed across the country.[121]

In 1927 Newark became center stage. On March 23, 1927 Louis Gah Fung of the On Leung organization was shot 27 times by a Hip Sing member in 7 Mulberry Arcade off of Mulberry Street. Five others were killed across the country before a truce was negotiated.[122]

This activity did nothing to help the image of the Chinese in the American press. A description of "the real Chinatown" stated that "The section always has lived in quiet fashion and there is passive unfriendliness to whites." The passiveness would give way to

---

[120] *Newark Evening News* October 13, 1924.

[121] *Newark Evening News* October 13, 1924, March 24, 1927.

[122] *Newark Evening News* June 8, 1958, Newark Evening News, March 24, 1927.

aggression if an outsider tried to enter the Arcade. Guards stood at the door to keep the curious away, but they don't resist the police. It was acknowledged that the area also included "the easy going Chinese who live in the section just to be with their compatriots." [123]

In 1932 Police raids finally ended the gambling activity which stopped the flow of winnings into the Chinatown community. The loss of this stream of money flowing into the local economy had a telling effect. Of the fourteen Chinese restaurants located in the Chinatown area in 1932, only nine remained in 1933.[124] With the departure of illicit activity, "the once forbidden Arcade" became "as safe for the curious stroller as his own backyard."[125]

However, the one event that would truly change the image of Chinese-Americans was the Second World War. China's alliance with the United States during World War II was the most significant factor in improving American attitudes towards the Chinese. News coverage of the war with Japan lifted the image of China and her citizens from uncivilized heathens to heroic patriots. With the help of the Republic of China's American educated first lady, Soong Mei-ling, the Chinese government was able to convince the American public that China was

---

[123] *Newark Evening News*, March 24, 1927, In this article, the dimensions of Chinatown are described as "Mulberry street (sic) from Lafayette street (sic) a little beyond Green street (sic) ; Mulberry Arcade running T-like off Mulberry street (sic) and a few buildings on Columbia. . ."

[124] City Directories 1932, 1933-1934.

[125] Newark News January 26, 1933.

an important part of the world order. This combined with the increase in the American Born Chinese population, allowed Chinese-Americans to be viewed as part of the American mosaic. But it did not stop the wilting of Newark's Chinatown.

In 1931, "Social workers in the district along Mulberry street [sic] reported . . . that the Chinese were leaving the city, that old Chinatown was passing."[126] The final gambling raid in 1932 along with the effects of the Great Depression accelerated this tread causing a precipitous drop in the Chinese population of the area.[127] Newark's Chinatown began a decades' long slide into oblivion.

"The bulk of Newark's Chinese went to New York where the neighborhood of Mott and Pell Streets was developing as the East's No. 1 center of Chinese-American life."[128] Some hope of revival appeared in 1941, with a report of the "Boom Restored to Chinatown After 10 Years." Unlike the previous prosperity of the district, this time it was chiefly the restaurants that attracted patrons. Ten "lean" years of depression had tarnished the district's imagine, but it was now "blossoming again like a parched garden blessed with rain."[129] It was a short lived revival. With the entry of the United States into

---

[126] *Newark Evening News*, February 2, 1931.

[127] The police raided the Mulberry Arcade 42 times in three years in the late 1920's and early 1930's, but most of these raids appear to have been for narcotics.

[128] *The Newark Star Ledger*, October 14, 1956.

[129] *The Newark Star Ledger,* October 17, 1941.

World War II, the lean years returned. When the nation emerged from the war, it had changed. The suburbs now beckoned returning veterans and the pent up savings of people over the war years allowed them to answer the call. Many Chinese moved to the suburbs of Northern New Jersey and opened restaurants. By 1958 there were an estimated 250 Chinese restaurants throughout the state.[130]

Although the closing of gambling had an immediate effect, the demise of Chinatown was probably inevitable. The combination of it being primarily a bachelor community and the fact that any children that did grow up along Mulberry Street would want to follow the America dream was insurmountable. "Second generation Chinese Americans, free of the language burden faced by their parents . . . turned to the fields of medicine, engineering, and other crafts and skills."[131]

As for the hand laundry business, it too gradually disappeared from the scene. Laundry men grew old. It was a bitter existence that they would not have wanted to pass on.[132] The need for the service declined as modern washers and dryers along with permanent press clothing came on the market.[133] All these factors led to the once ubiquitous Chinese hand laundry fading from the American landscape.

---

[130] *Newark Evening News*, February 16, 1958.

[131] *Newark Evening News*, February 16, 1958.

[132] See the description of the Chinese laundrymen's life in Iris Chang's *The Chinese in America*, pages 168 - 172.

[133] According to Wikipedia, electric laundry machines were common even

Reports on how large the Newark community was are all over the map. Newspaper reports claimed a population of more than 200 in 1892. A 1923 report said the population had been cut in half, but did not give the actual number. An article in 1941 stated that there had been a thirty year decline in the Chinatown population, from 800 to less than 100. In an interview given in 1947, a spokesman for the president of a newly opened social club said the Chinese population in the area of Mulberry Street and Lafayette Street had been between 1,500 and 2,000 before declining to about 400. Reports in 1956 and 1958 put the figures at 1,000 at the beginning of 1933, with population dropping to about 300 in six months. By 1965 it was claimed that the Chinese population for the entire city had been 3,000 in 1922, "most of them centered in the old Chinatown quarter . . .." [134]

No sources for these figures were given and there is no way to verify the numbers, many of which appeared decades after the fact. Census figures are much lower even taking into account the undercounting of minority groups that prevails with each census. (see appendix) By the 1950's that number had dropped to 200. The Mulberry Arcade was torn down in 1958. There were no Chinese

---

before World War II. Manufacture of the machines was suspended during the war, but quickly picked up. The first clothes dryer was introduced in 1938. For those who could not afford or did not have room for a washer, the first laundromat was opened in Fort Worth, Texas in 1934. 1953 saw the introduction of Wash and Wear shirts.

[134] *Newark Evening News* January 30, 1892, May 5, 1923, *The Star Ledger*, October 17, 1941, *The Star* Ledger, October 14, 1956, Newark *Evening News*, February 16, 1958, *The Star Ledger,* February 6, 1965.

residents in the two buildings when the tenants were evicted.[135] The 1966 Newark population was reported as 50 families city wide and nostalgia had replaced the condemnations of earlier times. One opinion piece lamented that "Newark has been the poorer and sadder for the loss of a wonderful group that contributed to the culture and economy of the city, not to mention the loss of a very law abiding group of people."[136]

The dramatic change in attitude towards the Chinese in New Jersey followed a winding path through exclusion, gambling and narcotic raids, tong wars, and two World Wars. This change brought an end to the Exclusion Acts in 1943. However, because of the passage of immigration reform in 1924 which sought to maintain the 1890 ethnic makeup of the United States, the number of Chinese who could legally enter the country was set at 105. At the end of the war, the War Brides Act allowed about 9,000 Chinese women into the country, greatly improving the male to female ratio of the community.[137] Then in 1952, as a result of the communist victory on

---

[135] *Newark Evening News* June 8, 1958.

[136] *The Newark Star Ledger* February 6, 1965. Contrast this with an article in the *Newark Evening News* that appeared on May 19, 1893. "Poor John Chinaman! The Geary law sits on him, the Supreme Court decision steps upon him, and now a hospital in this State of New Jersey offends him by refusing to admit him. Poor John Chinaman!"

[137] In January of 1945, a reporter was told that there would be no Chinese New Year celebration in Newark. One of the reasons given was "Too many Newark Chinese boys have gone to war." Some of these boys brought back brides from Hong Kong and China.

mainland China, the McCarren-Walter Immigration Act admitted 30,000 Chinese with immigration status. 5,000 were stranded scholars, among whom there were two future Noble Prize in physics laureates, Yang Chen Ning and Lee Tsung Dao, as well as I.M. Pei and An Wang.[138]

In 1965 Congress passed what would prove to be the most sweeping immigration reform for the Chinese since the Exclusion Act of 1882. The Hart-Cellar Act provided for 20,000 legal immigrants from every country outside the Western Hemisphere. This gave China, at that time the Republic of China on Taiwan, 20,000 immigration slots. 600 additional slots were given to Hong Kong. Many of these were taken by graduate students who chose to remain in the US after completing their degrees. 97% of the 150,000 Taiwanese students who came to study in America between the mid-60's and the mid-80's remained in the States by converting their F-1 student status into immigrant status. This figure gradually decreased as Taiwan's economy took off. By the late 80's and into the 90's Taiwanese graduate students were returning to their home more frequently because of the increased career opportunities available there. Author Peter Kwong used the terms of "uptown Chinese" and "downtown Chinese" to differentiate between the highly educated Chinese-Americans living in upper Manhattan and the less educated laboring

---

[138] *The New Chinatown p* 20, 59-60, Kwong, Peter, *The Chinese in America*, Chang, Iris p. 215-235.

Chinese-Americans in lower Manhattan. These students-turned-immigrants are the core of the uptown Chinese.[139]

US foreign policy continued to affect the number of Chinese coming into America. When President Carter moved official recognition from the Republic of China to the People's Republic of China, immigration quotas were set for both countries in effect doubling the number of Chinese immigrants allowed into the country. The increase in the Chinese-American population "has been extremely rapid since 1979." Ethnic Chinese were not included in the numbers given to Taiwan, China, and Hong Kong. Even though ethnic Chinese immigrants from Southeast Asia call themselves Chinese, US immigration law considers them citizens of the country they are emigrating from. This ensures that the number of people of Chinese extraction will be understated.

The effect on New Jersey's Chinese population numbers has been dramatic. Prior to the repeal of the Exclusion Act, the census enumerated 1,200 Chinese living within the confines of the Garden State. This number gradually increased to 23,400 by 1980. 1990 saw the figure jump to 59,084, a 252% increase in just one decade. By 2010 the number of New Jersey residents who claimed Chinese ancestry had climbed to 134,442. These figures would be a minimum considering the propensity to undercount the immigrant population.

---

[139] *The New Chinatown*, p. 59-62, Peter Kwong, *The Chinese Americans*, Iris Chang, p. 283-311, p353-354 footnotes.

Nationally the 2017 estimate of people claiming Chinese descent was 5,219,184.[140]

---

[140] *The New Chinatown*, p. 4, Peter Kwong, *Statistical Abstract of the United States* 1940, 1970-2010, https://factfinder.census.gov/faces/tableservices/jsf/pages/productview.xhtml?pid=ACS_16_1YR_S0201&prodType=table.

Appendixes

New Jersey Chinese Population on census.

1870 - 5 (3 in Ancestry but 38 born in China)

1880 - 170 (177 in Ancestry)

1890 - 608 (4 female)

1900 - 1,393 (1,335 in Ancestry, with 18 in Newark Navy Station)

1910 - 1,139 (1,113 in Ancestry)

1920 - 1,190 (1,293 in Ancestry, 296 in Newark w/27 females)

1930 - 1,783 (1,850 in Ancestry, 669 in Newark w/50 females)

1940 - 1,200 (1,420 in Ancestry, 298 in Newark w/82 females)

1950 - 3,815

1960 - 1,818

1970 - 9,233

1980 - 23,400

1990 - 59, 084 (54,338 from Mainland and 4,746 from Taiwan) 252% increase

2000 - 100,355 (94,476 from Mainland and 5,879 from Taiwan) 170% increase

2010 - 134,442

County	1900	1910	1920	1930	1940
Atlantic	43	45	34	48	51
Bergen	56	58	68	96	87
Burlington	30	15	17	21	13
Camden	78	68	61	73	65
Cumberland	5	3	5	7	5
Essex	364	340	485	813	400
Gloucester	2	8	7	13	2
Hudson	333	269	186	283	222
Hunterdon	5	8	4	3	0
Mercer	58	30	66	50	37
Middlesex	34	33	41	45	19
Monmouth	59	37	63	56	30
Morris	35	22	22	49	189
Ocean	10	10	11	10	6
Passaic	141	96	84	97	83
Salem	6	4	8	9	3
Somerset	13	9	9	5	3
Sussex	4	2	2	3	3
Union	53	53	64	104	62
Warren	3	1	3	0	10

Total Newark Population: Chinese Population:

1870 - 105,059   2 (Henrietta (30) & Henry (8) Day
                                   apparently adopted by Days)
1880 - 136,508   14
1890 - 181,830   (Detailed census figures lost to fire)
1900 - 246,070   255
1910 - 347,469   259
1915 (Jersey Census)   240
1920 - 414,524   296[141]
1930 - 442,337   669
1940 - 429,760   298

Chinese Population in other New Jersey Cities 1900-1940:

	1900	1910	1920	1930	1940
Jersey City	193	127	78	159	98
New Brunswick	16	23	17	15	10
Trenton	51	26	58	33	13
Atlantic City	39	69	31	44	44

---

[141] The City and County figures are from Ancestry.com searches. When I did the Ancetry.com search, it gave me a figure of 420 Chinese, but as I browsed through the names I found - 124 non-Chinese mixed in. I subtracted these from the Chinese.

Chinese Laundries in Newark City Directories

1880 - 4	1895 - 85	1920 - 132	1943 - 121
1881 - 15	1901 - 139	1922 - 123	1951 - 95
1886 - 46	1904 - 121	1923 - 129	1955 - 90
1890 - 45	1906 - 134	1924 - 132	1957 - 81
1891 - 61	1907 - 131	1929 - 143	
1892 - 77	1908 - 130	1932 - 140	
1893 - 93	1910 - 132	1933 - 140	
1894 - 117	1913 - 135	1935 - 131	

Chinese Restaurants in Newark

1895 - 1	1910 - 10	1932 - 19
1901 - 3	1913 - 6	1933 - 12
1904 - 2	1920 - 13	1935 - 17[142]
1906 - 9	1922 - 15	1943 - 15
1907 - 7	1923 - 21	1951 - 14
1908 - 7	1924 - 18	1955 - 10

---

[142] From 1935 on there were more Chinese restaurants outside the area of Chinatown than in it (7 inside, 8 outside). Contrast this to 1924 when there was only 1 Chinese restaurant outside of the area (17 inside, 1 outside).

Chinese Grocery/Tea Stores in Newark

1895 - 1	1906 - 3	1910 - 3	1922 - 6	1935 - 6
1901 - 1	1907 - 3	1913 - 5	1923 - 14	1951 - 2
1904 - 4	1908 - 3	1920 - 2	1924 - 12	

Bibliography

Newspapers

Jersey City American Standard, January 20, 1873.

Jersey City Evening Courier, September 22, 23, 1870.

New York Times, December 20, 21, 26, 1872; August 8, 1873; February 16, 1874; June 13, 1876; March 19,1877; August 8, 1880; February 19, 1882; February 7, 8,1883; January 28, 1884; December 8, 18, 1884; February 16, 1885; February 13, 1888.

New York Herald, September 23, 1870.

New York Tribune, August 21, 1875, September 6, 1875, June 21, 1885.

New York World, September 29, 1870.

Newark Morning Register, December 18, 19, 27, 29, 30, 31, 1884.

Paterson Press, February 6, 1875.

Sussex Register, October 20, 1870.

Newark Evening News, January 28, 1884; December 17, 18 1884; February 16, 1885; July 17, 1886; September 13, 1886; October 19, 1886; January 30; March 5; June 1, 7, 15, 16, 19, 25, ; July 7, 12, 13, 17, 23,28; August 16; September 13; October 19, 25; November 2, 13, 29; December 10, 11, 15, 1886, January 30, 1892, May 5, 1923, October13, 1924. March 24, 1927, June 21, 1930, February 2, 1931, January 26, 1933, October 17, 1941, February 16, 1958, June 8, 1958..

Newark Daily Journal, September 19, 21, 22, 24, 26, 28, 29, 30, 1870; October 3, 10, 13, 18, 20, 21, 22, 26, 28, 31, 1870; November 3, 4, 8, 9, 10, 17, 30, 1870; February 2, 18, 20, 1871; June 6, 1871; October 23, 24, 1871; December 23, 27, 1871; May 5, 22; October 18, 21, 1872; June 20, 1873; August 4, 15, 1873; November 7, 14, 1873; January 17, 1874; April 7,

85

8, 10, 11, 1874; October 5, 1874; February 5, 8, 1875; May 28, 1875; June 9, 1875; September 10, 1875; December 24, 1875; September 21, 1876.

Newark Daily Advertiser, September 22, 28, 29, 1870; October 4, 1870; November 22, 1870; February 17,1871; April 6, 1871; May 16, 1871; July 14, 15, 1871; May 15, 1872; August 30, 1872; September 2, 23, 28, 1872; November 29, 1872; December 5, 1872; January 20,1873; June 1, 1875; June 9, 1875; February 13, 1877; February 4, 1881; February 18, 1882; February 7, 8, 1883; December 18, 1884.

Newark Evening Courier, September 17, 21, 23, 28,29, 1870; October 1, 14,1870; November 14, 21, 1870; February 2, 18, 1871; May 17, 1871; June 6, 19, 1871; July 14, 1871; October 23, 1871; August 12, 1872; May 24, 1873; April 7, 11, 1874; July 15, 16, 1874; September 5, 1874; October 5, 27, 1874; February 8, 1875; May 27, 28, 1875.

The Sentinel of Freedom, May 26, 1885; December 14, 1886.

Newark Sunday Call, October 9, 1932.

The Newark Star Ledger, October 14, 1956, February 6, 1965.

Books

Belleville Dutch Reformed Church, *The History of the Old Church in the Valley: The 275th Anniversary of the Belleville Dutch Reformed Church*, Privately Printed, 1979.

Chang, Iris, *The Chinese in America: A Narrative History*, New York: Viking Press, 2003.

Daniels, Roger, *Coming to America*, New York: Harper Perennial, 1991.

Deconde, Alexander, *A History of American Foreign Pol icy, Volume I: Growth to World Power (1700-1914), Third Edition.* New York: Charles Scribner's Sons, 1978.

Hsu, Immanuel C.Y., *The Rise of Modern China, 3rd Edition*, New York: Oxford University Press, 1983.

Kwong, Peter, *The New Chinatown*, New York, Hill and Wong, 1987.

Holbrook City Directories, *Holbrook's City Directory, Newark, New Jersey*, Holbrook City Directories, Inc., Newark, New Jersey, 1875-1886, Business Section.

The Price and Lee Co., *Newark City Directory*, Newark, NJ, 1913, 1920, 1922, 1923, 1924, 1932,1933/34, Business Section.

Government Documents

New Jersey State Census, Union Township, 1855.

United States Census, Union Township, New Jersey, 1860.

United States Census, Union Township, New Jersey, 1870.

United States Census, Union Township, Rutherford, New Jersey, 1880.

New Jersey State Census, Union Township, Rutherford, New Jersey, 1885.

Bergen County New Jersey Clerk, Registry Office, Deed Book 0-9.

Newark, New Jersey Police First Precinct Criminal Docket, April, 1874.

United States Census, Newark, New Jersey, 1870, 1880, 1900, 1910, 1920, 1930, 1940.

www.ingramcontent.com/pod-product-compliance
Lightning Source LLC
Chambersburg PA
CBHW032019040426
42448CB00006B/668